PRACTICE – ASSESS – DIAGNOSE

180 Days of
Spelling & Word Study
for First Grade

Author
Shireen Pesez Rhoades, M.A.Ed.

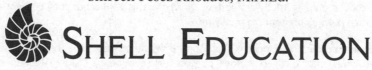
SHELL EDUCATION

Publishing Credits

Corinne Burton, M.A.Ed., *Publisher*
Conni Medina, M.A.Ed., *Editor in Chief*
Emily R. Smith, M.A.Ed., *Content Director*
Véronique Bos, *Creative Director*
Shaun N. Bernadou, *Art Director*
Bianca Marchese, M.S.Ed., *Editor*
Jess Johnson, *Graphic Designer*
Dani Neiley, *Assistant Editor*

Image Credits

All images are from iStock and/or Shutterstock.

Standards

© 2014 Mid-continent Research for Education and Learning
© Copyright 2010. National Governors Association Center for Best Practices and Council of Chief State School Officers.
All rights reserved.
© Copyright 2007–2018 Texas Education Agency (TEA). All rights reserved.
© 2007 Teachers of English to Speakers of Other Languages, Inc. (TESOL)
© 2014 Board of Regents of the University of Wisconsin System, on behalf of WIDA— www.wida.us.

Shell Education

A division of Teacher Created Materials
5301 Oceanus Drive
Huntington Beach, CA 92649-1030
www.tcmpub.com/shell-education

ISBN 978-1-4258-3309-1

©2019 Shell Educational Publishing, Inc.

Table of Contents

Introduction

180 Days of Spelling and Word Study provides the missing piece to today's language arts curriculum. Developed by a reading consultant with more than 20 years of classroom and literacy experience, this research-based program is easy to implement, simple to differentiate, and adaptable to any instructional model. The activities are straightforward and engaging. Most importantly, they address today's college and career readiness standards.

This book boosts students' spelling, vocabulary, and decoding skills by familiarizing them with common patterns in a logical, sequential format. Each five-day unit explores a new concept or letter pattern.

Goals of the Series

The first goal of the series is to build students' familiarity with common spelling patterns and rules. The scope and sequence has been designed using a developmental approach, taking into account students' predictive stages of spelling development. Units progress from basic letter sounds to challenging patterns and spiral from one year to the next.

A second goal is to strengthen decoding skills. When students spend a week or more immersed in a particular phonetic pattern, they start to notice and apply the pattern to their daily reading. This program's emphasis on common spelling patterns strengthens students' word-attack skills and helps them break large words into syllables and meaningful chunks.

Introduction (cont.)

Goals of the Series (cont.)

Vocabulary development is the third, and perhaps most critical, goal of the series. Tasks are meaning-based, so students cannot complete them successfully without some knowledge of the words' definitions or parts of speech. Additionally, activities are designed to deepen students' knowledge of targeted words by requiring them to manipulate synonyms, antonyms, and multiple meanings.

Structured Practice

To be successful in spelling, students must focus on the words, word parts, patterns, and definitions. For that reason, this series uses structured practice. Rather than changing the activities week-to-week, the daily activities are repeated throughout the 36 units. That way, students can focus on the words instead of learning how to complete the activities.

The following activities are used throughout this book:

Title of Activity	Description
Analogies	Students use a word bank to complete analogies.
Categories	Students sort words into categories.
Change a Letter	Students change a letter to create a new word.
Homophones	Students choose the correct homophones to complete sentences.
Inflectional Endings	Students add inflectional endings to given words.
Picture Match	Students match pictures to words.
Plural Practice	Students practice adding –s and –es to make words plural.
Sentence Completions	Students use a word bank to complete sentences.
Sentence Practice	Students practice writing sentences with spelling words.
Sentence Types	Students use given words to write statements and questions.
Synonyms and Antonyms	Students use a word bank to list synonyms or antonyms of given words.
Tapping Sounds	Students tap sounds out and write the letters they hear.
Turn the Question Around	Students use given words to answer questions in complete sentences.
Verb Tenses	Students practice present and past tense.
Word Sorts	Students sort words into categories.

How to Use This Book

180 Days of Spelling and Word Study is comprised of 36 units. Each unit revolves around a particular phonetic pattern and includes five separate activities. They can be assigned as homework or morning work, or they can be used as part of a word work rotation. Activities vary throughout each unit.

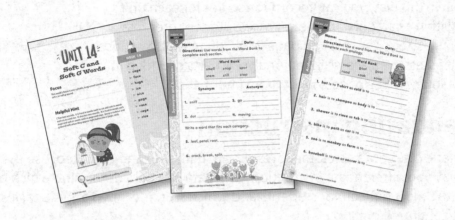

In this book, students will explore: long and short vowels, vowel teams, diphthongs, digraphs, hard/soft consonants, and *r*-controlled vowels. Students apply these patterns to two-syllable words with prefixes and predictable endings such as *–ing*, *–ed*, and *–s*. Students begin to explore unusual vowel teams and the many roles of the silent *e*. Common prefixes, suffixes, and homophones are studied as well.

Unit Assessments

A list of words is provided at the beginning of each unit. The words share a pattern that is reinforced in activities throughout the unit. You may choose to send the words home as part of a traditional study list. Additional spelling activities are provided on page 7 as well as in the Digital Resources. These activities can be specifically assigned, or the whole list can be sent home as a school-home connection.

However, in place of a typical spelling test, you are encouraged to administer the unit quizzes provided on pages 237–238. Each unit quiz contains two to three words and a dictation sentence. The individual words fit the unit pattern but have not been previously studied. Spelling the words correctly demonstrates that students have mastered the unit's spelling objectives and can apply them to daily work. Further, two to four words in the sentence dictation come from the study list. The rest of the sentence consists of high-frequency or review words. Dictation sentences measure how well students can spell target words in context, while attending to capitalization and punctuation rules.

How to Use This Book *(cont.)*

Unit Assessments *(cont.)*

The units are grouped into categories so you can diagnose how well students understand key phonetic patterns. By grouping these units together in this way, you can record the scores for each unit's assessment within a category and better assess student progress. See the Spelling Categories chart on page 239. You may also choose to record unit assessment scores in the Analysis Charts provided in the Digital Resources. See page 240 for more information.

Differentiating Instruction

Once a phonetic category's assessment results are gathered and analyzed, use the results to inform the way you differentiate instruction. The data can help determine which phonetic patterns are the most difficult for students and which students need additional instructional support and continued practice.

Whole-Class Support

The results of the diagnostic analysis may show that the entire class is struggling with certain phonetic patterns. If they have been taught in the past, this indicates that further instruction or reteaching is necessary. If these patterns have not been taught in the past, this data is a great preassessment and may demonstrate that students do not have a working knowledge of the weekly pattern. Thus, careful planning for reintroducing the words or patterns may be required.

Small-Group or Individual Support

The results of the diagnostic analysis may also show that an individual student or a small group of students is struggling with certain spelling patterns. If these patterns have been taught in the past, this indicates that further instruction or reteaching is necessary. Consider pulling these students aside to instruct them further while others are working independently. Students may also benefit from extra practice using spelling games or computer-based resources.

You can also use the results to help identify proficient individual students or groups of students who are ready for enrichment or above-level spelling instruction. These students may benefit from independent learning contracts or more challenging words. The Additional Spelling Activities chart has strong options to further challenge students (page 7 and in the Digital Resources).

Included in the Digital Resources are lists of words used in *180 Days of Spelling and Word Study* for grades K, 1, and 2. These lists can be used for differentiation.

How to Use This Book (cont.)

Additional Spelling Activities

The activities included here offer additional ways to practice the spelling words in each unit. They also make a great school-home connection!

Activity Name	Description
ABC Order	Write each word on a separate slip of paper. Mix up the slips of paper, and arrange them in ABC order.
ABCs	Practice writing uppercase and lowercase letters.
Air Spelling	Spell each word in the air using one or two fingers. Have a partner guess which word you spelled.
Best Writing	Write each spelling word two times in your best printing.
Cut Out Words	Cut out letters from newspapers or magazines, and use the letters to form the spelling words. Glue the words onto a sheet of paper.
Rainbow Spelling	Write each word with a crayon. Trace around the words in a different color crayon. Trace around both colors in a third color.
Shaving Cream Writing	Practice writing spelling words in shaving cream on your desk or in a baking tray.
Silly Spelling Story	Write a silly story that uses as many spelling words as possible.
Spelling Scramble	Write each spelling word on a separate index card. Cut apart the letters of each word. Place the letters for each word in a separate zip-top bag. Working with a partner, dump out the letters from one bag at a time and unscramble the words.

How to Use This Book (cont.)

Word Lists

This chart lists the words and phonetic patterns covered in each unit.

Unit	Words	Spelling Pattern
1	bag, cap, fan, jam, nap, pad, pan, rag, wax, yam	short *a* words
2	bib, dig, fin, kids, lips, pig, quit, ribs, six, zip	short *i* words
3	box, cop, fox, job, jog, log, mop, nod, pot, sob	short *o* words
4	bug, bun, cup, gum, jug, mud, nut, rug, sun, tub	short *u* words
5	bed, beg, hen, jet, leg, men, net, pen, said, web	short *e* words
6	bell, buzz, cuff, doll, fill, hill, kiss, miss, puff, yell	bonus letters
7	back, deck, duck, kick, lick, lock, neck, puck, sack, sock	−*ck* ending
8	chick, chin, chip, dish, fish, rash, rich, shell, shin, ship	consonant digraphs *ch* and *sh*
9	bath, path, than, that, thick, thin, this, when, whip, with	consonant digraphs *th* and *wh*
10	ate, base, chase, late, same, save, shape, take, vase, whale	silent *e* with *a*
11	bike, bite, chime, dive, fire, hide, lime, pile, shine, time	silent *e* with *i*
12	cute, home, joke, mule, nose, robe, rose, rule, tube, use	silent *e* with *o* and *u*
13	come, done, give, gone, have, live, love, none, one, some	silent *e* rule breakers
14	ace, cage, face, huge, ice, nice, page, race, rage, rice	soft *c* and soft *g* words
15	blob, clap, class, cliff, flag, glad, glass, plus, sled, slip	initial blends with *l*
16	scab, skin, smell, snap, spot, stem, still, stop, stuff, swim	initial blends with *s*
17	brag, crab, dress, drop, frog, from, grass, grill, press, trap	initial blends with *r*
18	bay, day, hay, lay, may, pay, ray, say, they, way	long *a* vowel team *ay*
19	aid, aim, air, gain, hair, mail, paid, rain, tail, wait	long *a* vowel team *ai*
20	beak, each, eat, hear, leaf, mean, read, real, seal, teach	long *e* vowel team *ea*

28629—180 Days of Spelling and Word Study

How to Use This Book (cont.)

Unit	Words	Spelling Pattern
21	been, feed, feel, keep, meet, need, queen, seem, week, wheel	long *e* vowel team *ee*
22	boat, coat, foam, goal, goat, load, moan, road, soak, soap	long *o* vowel team *oa*
23	bow, foe, grow, low, mow, row, show, snow, toe, tow	long *o* vowel teams *oe* and *ow*
24	cry, die, dry, fly, lie, pie, sky, tie, try, why	long *i* patterns *ie* and *y*
25	fight, high, light, might, night, right, sigh, sight, thigh, tight	long *i* pattern *igh*
26	cool, food, loop, mood, moon, noon, pool, roof, room, soon	long *u* pattern *oo*
27	blue, chew, clue, dew, due, few, flew, glue, new, stew	long *u* vowel teams *ue* and *ew*
28	book, foot, full, good, look, pull, push, put, took, wood	words with schwa
29	about, couch, down, gown, how, loud, mouth, now, out, town	*ou* and *ow* diphthongs
30	boil, boy, coil, coin, foil, join, joy, oil, soil, toy	*oi* and *oy* diphthongs
31	ball, fall, jaw, lawn, loss, saw, talk, tall, toss, walk	words with /aw/ sound
32	are, arm, bar, cart, dark, hard, park, part, star, yard	*r*-controlled vowels with *ar*
33	born, cord, corn, for, fork, horn, more, port, sort, your	*r*-controlled vowels with *our*, *or*, and *ore*
34	bird, burn, dirt, firm, fur, girl, her, hurt, turn, word	*r*-controlled vowels with *er*, *ir*, and *ur*
35	bang, hang, hung, king, long, lungs, ring, sing, song, wing	–*ng* ending
36	bank, dunk, honk, junk, link, pink, sank, sink, tank, wink	–*nk* ending

Standards Correlations

Shell Education is committed to producing educational materials that are research and standards based. All products are correlated to the academic standards of all 50 states, the District of Columbia, the Department of Defense Dependent Schools, and the Canadian provinces.

How to Find Standards Correlations

To print a customized correlation report of this product for your state, visit **www.tcmpub.com/ administrators/correlations/** and follow the online directions. If you require assistance in printing correlation reports, please contact the Customer Service Department at 1-877-777-3450.

Purpose and Intent of Standards

The Every Student Succeeds Act (ESSA) mandates that all states adopt challenging academic standards that help students meet the goal of college and career readiness. While many states already adopted academic standards prior to ESSA, the act continues to hold states accountable for detailed and comprehensive standards.

Standards are designed to focus instruction and guide adoption of curricula. Standards are statements that describe the criteria necessary for students to meet specific academic goals. They define the knowledge, skills, and content students should acquire at each level. Standards are also used to develop standardized tests to evaluate students' academic progress. Teachers are required to demonstrate how their lessons meet state standards. State standards are used in the development of all Shell products, so educators can be assured they meet the academic requirements of each state.

College and Career Readiness

In this book, the following college and career readiness (CCR) standards are met: Uses conventional spelling for high-frequency and other studied words and for adding suffixes to base words; uses spelling patterns and generalizations; and consults reference materials, including beginning dictionaries, as needed to check and correct spellings.

McREL Compendium

Each year, McREL analyzes state standards and revises the compendium to produce a general compilation of national standards. In this book, the following standard is met: Uses conventions of spelling in written compositions.

TESOL and WIDA Standards

In this book, the following English language development standards are met: Standard 1: English language learners communicate for social and instructional purposes within the school setting. Standard 2: English language learners communicate information, ideas, and concepts necessary for academic success in the content area of language arts.

UNIT 1
Short A Words

Focus

This week's focus is consonant-vowel-consonant (CVC) words with short *a*.

Helpful Hint

Short *a* sounds a little different when it comes before *m* or *n*. Notice the nasal /*a*/ in words like *fan* and *jam*.

- ➤ **bag**
- ➤ **cap**
- ➤ **fan**
- ➤ **jam**
- ➤ **nap**
- ➤ **pad**
- ➤ **pan**
- ➤ **rag**
- ➤ **wax**
- ➤ **yam**

See page 7 for additional spelling activities.

Name: _____ **Date:** _____

Directions: Use the Word Bank to write a word for each picture.

Word Bank				
bag	cap	fan	jam	nap
pad	pan	wax	yam	

1.

_____

_____

2.

_____

_____

3.

_____

_____

4.

_____

_____

5.

_____

_____

6.

_____

_____

7.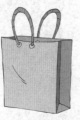

_____

_____

8.

_____

_____

9.

_____

_____

Picture Match

Name: _____ **Date:** _____

Directions: Say the word that names each picture. Tap out the sounds in the word. Write the letter that matches each sound in a separate box.

1.

2.

3.

4.

Directions: Write one of the words two times.

_____   _____

- - - - - - - - - - - - - - - -   - - - - - - - - - - - - - - - -

_____   _____

Name: _____ **Date:** _____

Directions: Look at both pictures. Say both words. Cross out the letter that changes. Write the second word.

1.

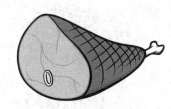

_____

‎- ‎- ‎- ‎- ‎- ‎- ‎-

_____

2.

_____

‎- ‎- ‎- ‎- ‎- ‎- ‎-

_____

3.

_____

‎- ‎- ‎- ‎- ‎- ‎- ‎-

_____

4.

_____

‎- ‎- ‎- ‎- ‎- ‎- ‎-

_____

Name: _____ **Date:** _____

Directions: Adding –s to the end of a word changes the word to mean *more than one*. The word becomes a plural. Write the plural words.

1.   cap   _____

_____

2.   yam   _____

_____

3.   fan   _____

_____

4.   pad   _____

_____

Name: _____ **Date:** _____

Directions: Write a sentence using each word.

Example: *cat*: My cat has black fur.

_____

1. *rag*: _____

_____

_ _

_____

2. *cap*: _____

_____

_ _

_____

3. *wax*: _____

_____

_ _

_____

UNIT 2
Short *I* Words

Focus

This week's focus is CVC words with short *i*.

Helpful Hint

Three words on this list are plurals (*kids, lips, ribs*). The –*s* on the end is a reminder that the word means more than one.

> **bib**
> **dig**
> **fin**
> **kids**
> **lips**
> **pig**
> **quit**
> **ribs**
> **six**
> **zip**

See page 7 for additional spelling activities.

Name: _____ **Date:** _____

Directions: Use the Word Bank to write a word for each picture.

Word Bank				
bib	dig	fin	kids	lips
pig	ribs	six	zip	

1.

_____

_____

2.

_____

_____

3.

_____

_____

4.

_____

_____

5.

_____

_____

6.

_____

_____

7.

_____

_____

8.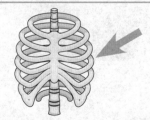

_____

_____

9.

_____

_____

Name: _____ **Date:** _____

Directions: Say the word that names each picture. Tap out the sounds in the word. Write the letter that matches each sound in a separate box.

1.

2.

3.

4.

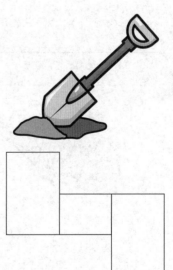

Directions: Write one of the words two times.

_____   _____

_ _ _ _ _ _ _ _ _ _ _ _ _   _ _ _ _ _ _ _ _ _ _ _ _ _

_____   _____

Name: _____ **Date:** _____

Directions: Look at both pictures. Say both words. Cross out the letter that changes. Write the second word.

1.

(p) (i) (g)

_____

- - - - - - - - - - -

_____

2.

(l) (i) (d) (s)

_____

- - - - - - - - - - -

_____

3.

(f) (a) (n)

_____

- - - - - - - - - - -

_____

4.

(s) (a) (x)

_____

- - - - - - - - - - -

_____

 28629—180 Days of Spelling and Word Study

Name: _____ **Date:** _____

Directions: Write each word with an *–s* on the end to show it means more than one. Write the plural words.

1. kid _____

2. bib _____

3. fin _____

4. pig _____

Plural Practice

Name: _____ **Date:** _____

Directions: Write a sentence using each word.

Example: *lid*:   The pot is missing a lid.
_____

_____

1. *six*: _____

_____

_____

_____

2. *quit*: _____

_____

_____

_____

3. *kids*: _____

_____

_____

UNIT 3
Short O Words

Focus

This week's focus is CVC words with short *o*.

Helpful Hint

Two words on this list end with –*x* (*box*, *fox*). When a word ends with –*x*, make it plural by adding –*es* instead of –*s*. Listen for the extra vowel sound at the end.

- box
- cop
- fox
- job
- jog
- log
- mop
- nod
- pot
- sob

🔍 See page 7 for additional spelling activities.

Name: _____ **Date:** _____

Directions: Use the Word Bank to write a word for each picture.

Picture Match

Word Bank				
box	dog	dots	fox	jog
log	mop	pot	rod	

1.

_____
_____
_____

2.

_____
_____
_____

3.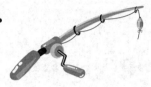

_____
_____
_____

4.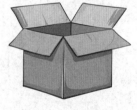

_____
_____
_____

5.

_____
_____
_____

6.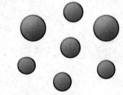

_____
_____
_____

7.

_____
_____
_____

8.

_____
_____
_____

9.

_____
_____
_____

Name: _____ **Date:** _____

Directions: Say the word that names each picture. Tap out the sounds in the word. Write the letter that matches each sound in a separate box.

1.

2.

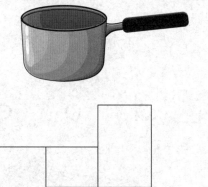

3.

4.

Directions: Write one of the words two times.

_____   _____

_____   _____

Name: _____ **Date:** _____

Directions: Look at both pictures. Say both words. Cross out the letter that changes. Write the second word.

1.

(d) (o) (g)

_____

_____

2.

(c) (a) (p)

_____

_____

3.

(p) (i) (t)

_____

_____

4.

(m) (a) (p)

_____

_____

Name: _____ **Date:** _____

Directions: Write each word with an –s on the end to show it means more than one. If a word ends with x, make it plural by adding –es.

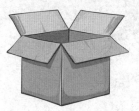 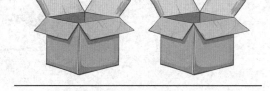

1.   box   _____

2.   fox   _____

3.   pot   _____

4.   mop   _____

Sentence Practice

Name: _____ **Date:** _____

Directions: Write a sentence using each word.

Example: *fog*: The fog is thick today.

_____

_____

1. *nod*: _____

_____

_____

_____

2. *job*: _____

_____

_____

_____

3. *sob*: _____

_____

_____

UNIT 4
Short U Words

Focus

This week's focus is CVC words with short *u*.

Helpful Hint

Some sight words, such as *of*, are rule breakers because the letters don't make their usual sounds. They are important words to know, so students should memorize them.

- bug
- bun
- cup
- gum
- jug
- mud
- nut
- rug
- sun
- tub

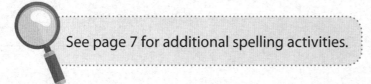

See page 7 for additional spelling activities.

Picture Match

Name: _____ **Date:** _____

Directions: Use the Word Bank to write a word for each picture.

Word Bank				
bug	bun	cup	gum	jug
mud	rug	sun	tub	

1.

_____

2.

_____

3.

_____

4.

_____

5.

_____

6.

_____

7.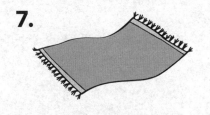

_____

8.

_____

9.

_____

Name: _____ **Date:** _____

Directions: Say the word that names each picture. Tap out the sounds in the word. Write the letter that matches each sound in a separate box.

1.

2.

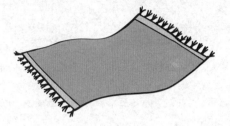

3.

4.

Directions: Write one of the words two times.

_____   _____

_____   _____

Name: _____ Date: _____

Directions: Look at both pictures. Say both words.
Cross out the letter that changes. Write the
second word.

1.

（b）（u）（g）

_____

- - - - - - - - - - -

_____

2.

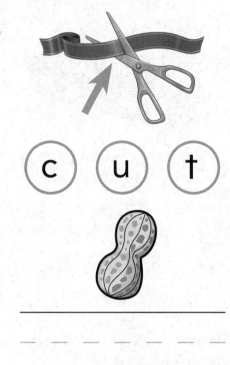

（c）（u）（t）

_____

- - - - - - - - - - -

_____

3.

（b）（u）（n）

_____

- - - - - - - - - - -

_____

4.

（c）（a）（p）

_____

- - - - - - - - - - -

_____

Name: _____ **Date:** _____

Directions: Write each word with an –s on the end to show it means more than one.

1. bus
_____

2. cup
_____

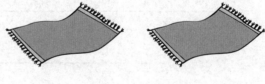

3. rug
_____

4. jug
_____

Plural Practice

Name: _____ **Date:** _____

Directions: Write a sentence using each word.

Example: *tug*:   My dog tugs on her leash.

_____

1. *gum*: _____

_____

_____

_____

2. *mud*: _____

_____

_____

_____

3. *fun*: _____

_____

_____

UNIT 5
Short E Words

Focus

This week's focus is CVC words with short *e*.

Helpful Hint

Said is a sight word that needs to be memorized. It has the short *e* sound but is spelled with *ai*. It cannot be tapped out because the *a* and *i* do not make their usual sounds.

- ➤ **bed**
- ➤ **beg**
- ➤ **hen**
- ➤ **jet**
- ➤ **leg**
- ➤ **men**
- ➤ **net**
- ➤ **pen**
- ➤ **said**
- ➤ **web**

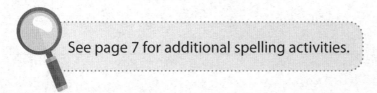

See page 7 for additional spelling activities.

Picture Match

Name: _____ **Date:** _____

Directions: Use the Word Bank to write a word for each picture.

Word Bank

bed	beg	hen	jet	leg
men	net	pen	web	

1.

_____

_____

2.

_____

_____

3.

_____

_____

4.

_____

_____

5.

_____

_____

6.

_____

_____

7.

_____

_____

8.

_____

_____

9.

_____

_____

Name: _____ **Date:** _____

Directions: Say the word that names each picture. Tap out the sounds in the word. Write the letter that matches each sound in a separate box.

1.

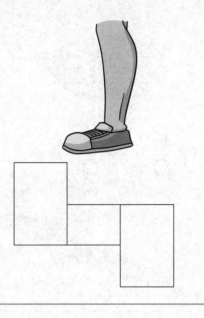

2.

3.

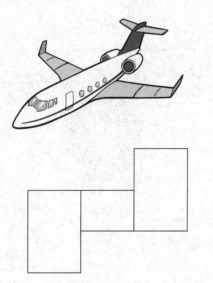

4.

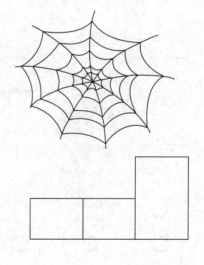

Directions: Write one of the words two times.

_____ _____

_ _ _ _ _ _ _ _ _ _ _ _   _ _ _ _ _ _ _ _ _ _ _ _

_____ _____

Change a Letter

Name: _____ **Date:** _____

Directions: Look at both pictures. Say both words. Cross out the letter that changes. Write the second word.

1.

(n) (e) (t)

_____

- - - - - - - - - - - - - - - - -

_____

2.

(p) (a) (n)

_____

- - - - - - - - - - - - - - - - -

_____

3.

(b) (e) (g)

_____

- - - - - - - - - - - - - - - - -

_____

4.

(B) (e) (n)

10

_____

- - - - - - - - - - - - - - - - -

_____

Name: _____ **Date:** _____

Directions: Use a word from the Word Bank for each analogy.

Word Bank

bed	jet	leg
men	pen	web

1. **bird** is to **nest** as **spider** is to _____

2. **moms** is to **women** as **dads** is to _____

3. **hand** is to **arm** as **foot** is to _____

4. **water** is to **boat** as **sky** is to _____

5. **sit** is to **chair** as **lay** is to _____

6. **lead** is to **pencil** as **ink** is to _____

Sentence Practice

Name: _____ **Date:** _____

Directions: Write a sentence using each word.

Example: *red*:   Stop signs are red.

_____

_____

1. *said*: _____

_____

_____

_____

_____

2. *net*: _____

_____

_____

_____

_____

3. *beg*: _____

_____

_____

UNIT 6
Bonus Letters

Focus

This week's focus is one-syllable, short vowel words that end with –*ff*, –*ll*, –*ss*, or –*zz*.

Helpful Hint

Some letters don't like to stay by themselves at the end of a word, so they have a bonus letter to keep them company. Letters that follow the bonus rule are *f, l, s,* and *z* (*puff, hill, kiss, buzz*). Notice they only get a bonus letter when they appear after a short vowel at the end of a word or syllable.

- ➤ **bell**
- ➤ **buzz**
- ➤ **cuff**
- ➤ **doll**
- ➤ **fill**
- ➤ **hill**
- ➤ **kiss**
- ➤ **miss**
- ➤ **puff**
- ➤ **yell**

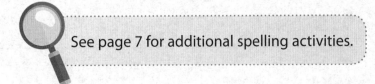

See page 7 for additional spelling activities.

Picture Match

Name: _____ **Date:** _____

Directions: Use the Word Bank to write a word for each picture.

Word Bank				
bell	buzz	cuff	doll	hill
kiss	puff	well	yell	

1.

_____

2.

_____

3.

_____

4.

_____

5.

_____

6.

_____

7.

_____

8.

_____

9.

_____

Name: _____ **Date:** _____

Directions: Say the word that names each picture. Tap out the sounds in the word. Write the letter that matches each sound in a separate box. If two letters work together to make one sound, write both letters in the same box.

1.

2.

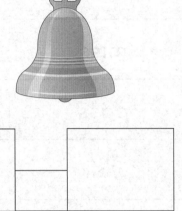

3.

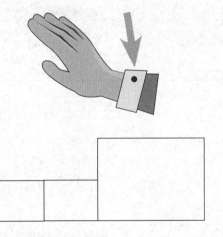

4.

Directions: Write one of the words two times.

_____   _____

_____   _____

Name: _____ **Date:** _____

Directions: Add –ed to each word.

Present Tense (Now I...)	Past Tense (Yesterday I...)
fill	
miss	
pass	
yell	
buzz	
kiss	
puff	
toss	

Adding –ed shows that something already happened. It is in the past tense. Notice that the –ed ending sometimes sounds like /t/ and sometimes sounds like /d/.

Verb Tenses

Name: _____ **Date:** _____

Directions: Write the past tense of each word.

Present Tense (Now I...)	Past Tense (Yesterday I...)
hide	
feed	
do	
sit	
have	
run	
bite	
get	

 Some words don't follow the *-ed* rule. They look and sound like a whole new word when they change to the past tense.

Name: _____ **Date:** _____

Analogies

Directions: Use a word from the Word Bank to complete each analogy.

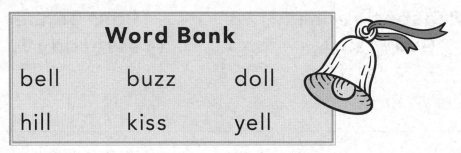

Word Bank

| bell | buzz | doll |
| hill | kiss | yell |

1. **big** is to **mountain** as **small** is to _____

2. **bang** is to **drum** as **ring** is to _____

3. **bird** is to **sing** as **bee** is to _____

4. **real** is to **baby** as **pretend** is to _____

5. **soft** is to **whisper** as **loud** is to _____

6. **arms** is to **hug** as **lips** is to _____

UNIT 7
–ck Ending

Focus

This week's focus is one-syllable, short vowel words that end with –ck.

Helpful Hint

A digraph is a pair of letters that works together to make one sound. The *ck* digraph says /k/. Notice that –*ck* only appears at the end of a word or syllable. Also, it only follows a single vowel that makes a short vowel sound (*ack, eck, ick, ock, uck*).

- ➤ **back**
- ➤ **deck**
- ➤ **duck**
- ➤ **kick**
- ➤ **lick**
- ➤ **lock**
- ➤ **neck**
- ➤ **puck**
- ➤ **sack**
- ➤ **sock**

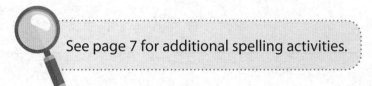

See page 7 for additional spelling activities.

Picture Match

Name: _____ **Date:** _____

Directions: Use the Word Bank to write a word for each picture.

Word Bank				
back	duck	kick	lock	neck
puck	rocks	sack	sock	

1.

_____

_____

2.

_____

_____

3.

_____

_____

4.

_____

_____

5.

_____

_____

6.

_____

_____

7.

_____

_____

8.

_____

_____

9.

_____

_____

Name: _____ **Date:** _____

Directions: Say the word that names each picture. Tap out the sounds in the word. Write the letter that matches each sound in a separate box. If two letters work together to make one sound, write both letters in the same box.

1.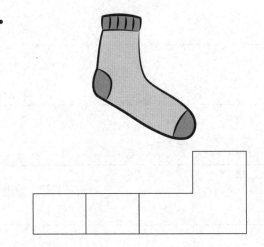

2.

3.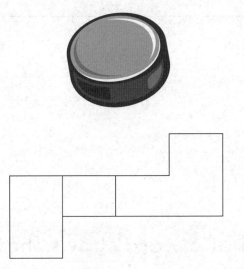

4.

Directions: Write one of the words two times.

_____   _____

_____   _____

Name: _____ **Date:** _____

Directions: Add *-ed* to each word.

Present Tense (Now I...)	Past Tense (Yesterday I...)
pack	
kick	
lick	
tuck	
lock	
pick	
duck	
peck	

Adding *-ed* to the end of a word shows that something already happened. If something already happened, it is in the past tense.

Name: _____ **Date:** _____

Directions: Study each example. Write the same kind of sentence using each word.

QUESTION **Ex.** *tuck*: Will you *tuck* me in?

_____

1. *back*: _____

_____

_____

2. *lock*: _____

_____

_____

STATEMENT **Ex.** *duck*: I fed a *duck* at the pond.

_____

3. *deck*: _____

_____

_____

4. *sock*: _____

_____

_____

Analogies

Name: _____ **Date:** _____

Directions: Use a word from the Word Bank to complete each analogy.

Word Bank

back	deck	duck
kick	lick	neck

1. **face** is to **front** as **tail** is to _____

2. **hand** is to **throw** as **foot** is to _____

3. **gum** is to **chew** as **lollipop** is to _____

4. **honk** is to **goose** as **quack** is to _____

5. **ring** is to **finger** as **necklace** is to _____

6. **house** is to **porch** as **ship** is to _____

UNIT 8
Consonant Digraphs *ch* and *sh*

- chick
- chin
- chip
- dish
- fish
- rash
- rich
- shell
- shin
- ship

Focus

This week's focus is one-syllable, short vowel words that start or end with *ch* or *sh*.

Helpful Hint

A digraph is a pair of letters that works together to make one sound. The *ch* digraph says /*ch*/. The *sh* digraph says /*sh*/. Notice that *ch* and *sh* digraphs can be found at the beginning or end of a word.

See page 7 for additional spelling activities.

Picture Match

Name: _____ **Date:** _____

Directions: Use the Word Bank to write a word for each picture.

Word Bank				
chick	chin	chip	dish	fish
rash	shell	shin	ship	

1.

_____

_____

2.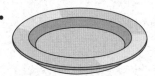

_____

_____

3.

_____

_____

4.

_____

_____

5.

_____

_____

6.

_____

_____

7.

_____

_____

8.

_____

_____

9.

_____

_____

Name: _____ **Date:** _____

Directions: Say the word that names each picture. Tap out the sounds in the word. Write the letter that matches each sound in a separate box. If two letters work together to make one sound, write both letters in the same box.

1.

2.

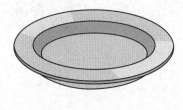

3.

4.

Directions: Write one of the words two times.

_____   _____

_____   _____

Name: _____ Date: _____

Directions: Adding –s to the end of a word changes the word to mean *more than one*. The word becomes a plural. Write each word with an –s on the end to show it means more than one.

1. chick

2. shell

 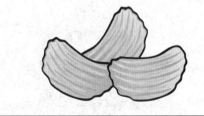

3. chip

4. ship

Name: _____ **Date:** _____

Directions: Study each example. Write the same kind of sentence using each word.

QUESTION **Ex.** *chop*:   Can you help *chop* wood?

_____

1. *rash*: _____

_____

_____

2. *dish*: _____

_____

_____

STATEMENT **Ex.** *chick*:   The baby *chick* is soft.

_____

3. *shell*: _____

_____

_____

4. *rich*: _____

_____

Analogies

Name: _____ **Date:** _____

Directions: Use a word from the Word Bank to complete each analogy.

Word Bank

chick	dish	fish
rash	shell	ship

_____

1. **water** is to **cup** as **food** is to _____

_____

2. **sky** is to **jet** as **sea** is to _____

_____

3. **cat** is to **kitten** as **hen** is to _____

_____

4. **bird** is to **feather** as **turtle** is to _____

_____

5. **sore** is to **sunburn** as **itchy** is to _____

_____

6. **robin** is to **bird** as **trout** is to _____

UNIT 9
Consonant Digraphs *th* and *wh*

Focus

This week's focus is one-syllable, short vowel words that start or end with *th* or *wh*.

Helpful Hint

A digraph is a pair of letters that works together to make one sound. The *th* digraph can make two sounds. It is soft and unvoiced in words such as *thin* but hard and voiced in words such as *this*. If you place your fingers on your throat as you say /*th*/ words, you can hear the difference between voiced and unvoiced sounds. The *wh* digraph says /*w*/. While most question words start with *wh* (*who*, *what*, *when*, *where*, *why*), there is no clear-cut rule to determine if other words start with *w* or *wh*.

> ➤ bath
> ➤ path
> ➤ than
> ➤ that
> ➤ thick
> ➤ thin
> ➤ this
> ➤ when
> ➤ whip
> ➤ with

See page 7 for additional spelling activities.

Name: _____ **Date:** _____

Directions: Use a word from the Word Bank to complete each sentence.

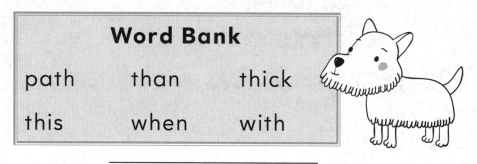

Word Bank		
path	than	thick
this	when	with

_____

1. My boots made a _____ in the snow.

_____

2. Will you play _____ me?

_____

3. Do you know _____ the food will be ready?

_____

4. I am bigger _____ my sister.

_____

5. My dog has lots of _____ fur.

_____

6. Where does _____ book belong?

Name: _____ **Date:** _____

Directions: Sort the *th* words by sound.

Word Bank				
bath	math	than	that	them
then	thick	thin	this	with

Soft, unvoiced *th*	Harder, voiced *th*

The *th* digraph can make two sounds. It is soft and unvoiced in words such as *thin*, but hard and voiced in words such as *they*. If you place your fingers on your throat as you say *th* words, you can hear the difference between voiced and unvoiced sounds.

Categories

Name: _____ **Date:** _____

Directions: A category is a group of words or things that go together. Use a word from the Word Bank to fit each category.

Word Bank					
math	path	thick	thin	this	when

1. road, trail, sidewalk, _____

2. reading, science, art, _____

3. skinny, lean, slender, _____

4. those, that one, these, _____

5. wide, chunky, big, _____

6. who, what, where, why, _____

Name: _____ **Date:** _____

Directions: Study each example. Write the same kind of sentence using each word.

QUESTION **Ex.** *that*: Is *that* your bike?

_____

1. *when*: _____

_____

_____

_____

2. *with*: _____

_____

_____

_____

STATEMENT **Ex.** *thick*: I got a *thick* slice of cake.

_____

3. *path*: _____

_____

_____

_____

4. *than*: _____

_____

_____

_____

Sentence Types

Name: _____ **Date:** _____

Directions: Use a word from the Word Bank to complete each analogy.

Analogies

Word Bank		
bath	math	path
thick	thin	when

_____

- - - - - - - - - - - - - - -

1. **stand** is to **shower** as **sit** is to _____

_____

- - - - - - - - - - - - - - -

2. **small** is to **big** as **thin** is to _____

_____

3. **letters** is to **reading** as **numbers** is to _____

- - - - - - - - - - - - - - -

4. **car** is to **road** as **bike** is to _____

_____

- - - - - - - - - - - - - - -

5. **tall** is to **short** as **fat** is to _____

_____

- - - - - - - - - - - - - - -

6. **school** is to **where** as **Friday** is to _____

UNIT 10
Silent E with A

Focus

This week's focus is one-syllable words with long *a* and silent *e*.

Helpful Hint

All the words on this list are "bossy e" words because the *e* at the end of the word jumps over the consonant and orders the vowel, "Say your name! Say your name!" Notice the long *a* sound in each word.

- ate
- base
- chase
- late
- same
- save
- shape
- take
- vase
- whale

See page 7 for additional spelling activities.

Name: _____ **Date:** _____

Directions: Use a word from the Word Bank to complete each sentence.

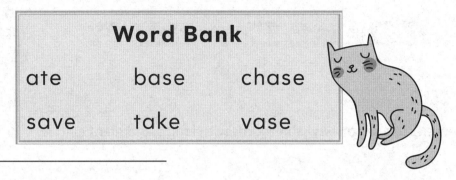

Word Bank

ate	base	chase
save	take	vase

_____
- - - - - - - - -

1. The _____ broke when it fell.

_____
- - - - - - -

2. I _____ the bus to school.

_____
- - - - - - -

3. I _____ pancakes for breakfast.

_____
- - - - - - -

4. I ran to first _____ after I hit the ball.

_____
- - - - - - -

5. I _____ money in my piggybank.

_____
- - - - - - -

6. My dog loves to _____ cats.

Name: _____ **Date:** _____

Directions: Say the word that names each picture. Tap out the sounds in the word. Write the letter that matches each sound in a separate box. Don't forget to write the silent *e* at the end.

1.

_____

- - -

2.

_____

- - -

3.

_____

- - -

4.

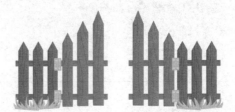

_____

- - -

Verb Tenses

Name: _____ **Date:** _____

Directions: Add –*ing* to each word.

Present Tense (Now I...)	Present Tense (I am...)
miss	
pass	
yell	
fill	

Directions: Add –*ing* to each word. Remember to drop the bossy *e* first.

Present Tense (Now I...)	Present Tense (I am...)
shape	
make	
chase	
save	

Adding –*ing* to the end of a word shows that something is happening right now. Did you know bossy *e* is afraid of –*ing*? When –*ing* shows up, bossy *e* says, "I'm outta here!"

Name: _____ **Date:** _____

Directions: Study each example. Write the same kind of sentence using each word.

QUESTION   **Ex.**   *base*:   Did he tag you at first *base*?

_____

1. *save*: _____

_____

_____

_____

2. *whale*: _____

_____

_____

_____

STATEMENT   **Ex.**   *chase*:   I had to *chase* the bus.

_____

3. *late*: _____

_____

_____

_____

4. *same*: _____

_____

Sentence Types

Analogies

Name: _____ **Date:** _____

Directions: Use a word from the Word Bank to complete each analogy.

Word Bank		
ate	cave	gate
male	rake	vase

1. **crumbs** is to **broom** as **leaves** is to _____

2. **fruit** is to **bowl** as **flowers** is to _____

3. **girl** is to **female** as **boy** is to _____

4. **do** is to **did** as **eat** is to _____

5. **house** is to **door** as **yard** is to _____

6. **bird** is to **nest** as **bat** is to _____

UNIT 11
Silent E with I

WEEK 11

- bike
- bite
- chime
- dive
- fire
- hide
- lime
- pile
- shine
- time

Focus

This week's focus is one-syllable words with long *i* and silent *e*.

Helpful Hint

All the words on this list are "bossy *e*" words because the *e* at the end of the word jumps over the consonant and orders the vowel, "Say your name! Say your name!" Notice the long *i* sound in each word.

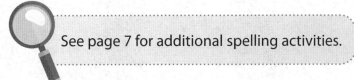

See page 7 for additional spelling activities.

Sentence Completions

Name: _____ **Date:** _____

Directions: Use a word from the Word Bank to complete each sentence.

Word Bank

bike	bite	hide
pile	shine	time

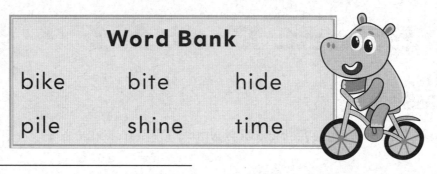

_____

1. Please _____ your papers in this box.

_____

2. My cat likes to _____ under the bed.

_____

3. I ride my _____ to school every day.

_____

4. Don't _____ your flashlight in my face.

_____

5. May I have a _____ of your cookie?

_____

6. It is _____ to clean your room now.

Name: _____ **Date:** _____

Directions: Say the word that names each picture. Tap out the sounds in the word. Write the letter that matches each sound in a separate box. Don't forget the silent *e* at the end.

1.

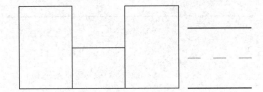

2.

3.

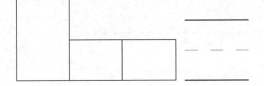

4.

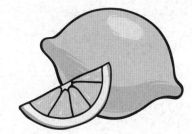

Verb Tenses

Name: _____ **Date:** _____

Directions: Add *–ing* to each word.

Present Tense (Now I...)	Present Tense (I am...)
hide	
dive	
ride	
bite	

Directions: Add *–ed* to each word.

Present Tense (Now I...)	Past Tense (Yesterday I...)
wipe	
whine	
pile	
dine	

Bossy *e* is afraid of *–ed*! When *–ed* shows up, bossy *e* says, "I'm outta here!"

Name: _____ **Date:** _____

Directions: Study each example. Write the same kind of sentence using each word.

QUESTION **Ex.** *hive:* Are there bees in the *hive*?

_____

1. *hide:* _____

_____

_____

_____

2. *time:* _____

_____

_____

STATEMENT **Ex.** *quite:* Dinner is not *quite* ready.

_____

3. *bike:* _____

_____

_____

_____

4. *fire:* _____

_____

_____

Name: _____ **Date:** _____

Directions: Use a word from the Word Bank to complete each analogy.

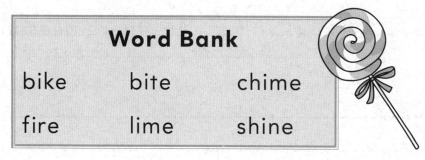

Word Bank

| bike | bite | chime |
| fire | lime | shine |

1. **drive** is to **car** as **ride** is to _____

2. **cold** is to **ice** as **hot** is to _____

3. **wind** is to **blow** as **sun** is to _____

4. **yellow** is to **lemon** as **green** is to _____

5. **alarm** is to **ring** as **bell** is to _____

6. **lollipop** is to **lick** as **candy bar** is to _____

UNIT 12
Silent E with O and U

- cute
- home
- joke
- mule
- nose
- robe
- rose
- rule
- tube
- use

Focus

This week's focus is one-syllable words with long *o* or *u* with silent *e*.

Helpful Hint

All the words on this list are "bossy *e*" words because the *e* at the end of the word jumps over the consonant and orders the vowel, "Say your name! Say your name!" Notice the long *o* or *u* sound in each word.

See page 7 for additional spelling activities.

© *Shell Education*

Sentence Completions

Name: _____ **Date:** _____

Directions: Use a word from the Word Bank to complete each sentence.

Word Bank		
joke	nose	robe
rose	rule	use

_____

- - - - - - - - - - -

1. His _____ made me laugh.

_____

- - - - - - - - - - -

2. Do you know how to _____ the toaster?

_____

- - - - - - - - - - -

3. A dog's _____ helps him find food.

_____

- - - - - - - - - - -

4. I wear my _____ when I get out of the bath.

_____

- - - - - - - - - - -

5. The _____ at school is no running in the hall.

_____

- - - - - - - - - - -

6. The red _____ bush bloomed overnight.

Name: _____ **Date:** _____

Directions: Say the word that names each picture. Tap out the sounds in the word. Write the letter that matches each sound in a separate box. Don't forget the silent *e* at the end.

1.

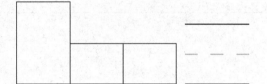

_ _ _ _ _

2.

_ _ _ _ _

3.

_ _ _ _ _

4.

_ _ _ _ _

Name: _____ **Date:** _____

Directions: Add –*ing* to each word.

Present Tense (Now I...)	Present Tense (I am...)
rule	
joke	
use	
doze	

Directions: Add –*ed* to each word.

Present Tense (Now I...)	Past Tense (Yesterday I...)
hope	
vote	
tune	
poke	

Verb Tenses

Name: _____ **Date:** _____

Directions: Study each example. Write the same kind of sentence using each word.

QUESTION **Ex.** *vote:* Who did you *vote* for?

_____

1. *mule:* _____

_____

_____

_____

2. *home:* _____

_____

_____

_____

STATEMENT **Ex.** *woke:* I *woke* up at 6:00 a.m.

_____

3. *rose:* _____

_____

_____

_____

_____

4. *cute:* _____

_____

_____

_____

Name: _____ **Date:** _____

Directions: Use a word from the Word Bank to complete each analogy.

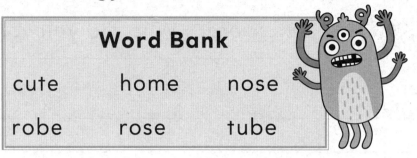

Word Bank

cute	home	nose
robe	rose	tube

1. **see** is to **eyes** as **smell** is to _____

2. **birds** is to **nest** as **family** is to _____

3. **monster** is to **ugly** as **baby** is to _____

4. **tree** is to **pine** as **flower** is to _____

5. **outside** is to **jacket** as **inside** is to _____

6. **jam** is to **jar** as **toothpaste** is to _____

UNIT 13
Silent E Rule Breakers

Focus

This week's focus is one-syllable words that end with silent *e* but do not contain a long vowel sound.

Helpful Hint

All the words on this list are bossy *e* rule breakers because the silent *e* does not jump over the consonant and tell the vowel to say its name. In some words, the silent *e* keeps *v* company at the end of a word (*give, have, live*). In other words, it changes the short *o* to a short *u* sound (*come, done, love, none, one, some*).

> ➤ come
> ➤ done
> ➤ give
> ➤ gone
> ➤ have
> ➤ live
> ➤ love
> ➤ none
> ➤ one
> ➤ some

See page 7 for additional spelling activities.

Sentence Completions

Name: _____ **Date:** _____

Directions: Use a word from the Word Bank to complete each sentence.

Word Bank

come	done	give
have	live	some

_____
- - - - - - - - - - -

1. May I have _____ milk?

_____
- - - - - - - - - - -

2. Can you _____ to my party next week?

_____
- - - - - - - - - - -

3. Do you _____ any pets?

_____
- - - - - - - - - - -

4. I am _____ with my homework.

_____
- - - - - - - - - - -

5. Did you _____ the dog more food?

_____
- - - - - - - - - - -

6. I _____ in a red house.

Name: _____ **Date:** _____

Directions: Use a word from the Word Bank to complete each section.

Word Bank

come	done	give	gone
have	love	none	some

Synonym	Antonym

1. missing _____

2. finished _____

3. a few _____

4. own _____

5. take _____

6. go _____

7. hate _____

8. all _____

Verb Tenses

Name: _____ **Date:** _____

Directions: Add *–ing* to each word. Remember to drop bossy *e* before you add *–ing*.

Present Tense (Now I...)	Present Tense (I am...)
come	
give	
have	
live	

Directions: Write the past tense of each word.

Present Tense (Now I...)	Past Tense (Yesterday I...)
ride	
give	
come	
have	

When a word ends with bossy *e*, drop the *e* before adding *–ed*. Some words don't follow the *–ed* rule. They look and sound like a whole new word when they change to the past tense.

Name: _____ **Date:** _____

Directions: Study each example. Write the same kind of sentence using each word.

QUESTION **Ex.** *some*: Can I have *some* help?

_____

1. *done*: _____

_____

_____

2. *come*: _____

_____

_____

STATEMENT **Ex.** *live*: I *live* on a farm.

_____

3. *one*: _____

_____

_____

4. *gone*: _____

_____

_____

Sentence Types

Name: _____ **Date:** _____

Directions: Use a word from the Word Bank to complete each analogy.

Analogies

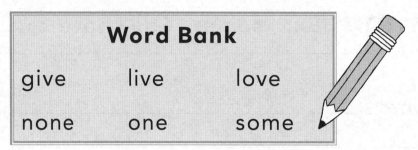

Word Bank		
give	live	love
none	one	some

1. **eyes** is to **two** as **nose** is to _____

2. **dislike** is to **hate** as **like** is to _____

3. **school** is to **learn** as **home** is to _____

4. **buy** is to **sell** as **take** is to _____

5. **a lot** is to **many** as **not any** is to _____

6. **to** is to **two** as **sum** is to _____

UNIT 14
Soft C and Soft G Words

Focus

This week's focus is one-syllable, long vowel words that end with a soft *c* or soft *g* sound.

Helpful Hint

C has two sounds. It is hard in words such as *cat* and soft in words such as *ice* and *rice*. *G* also has two sounds. It is hard in words such as *go* and soft in words such as *page* and *cage*. Bossy *e* makes *c* and *g* sound soft when they appear right before the *e* (*cage*, *race*).

- ace
- cage
- face
- huge
- ice
- nice
- page
- race
- rage
- rice

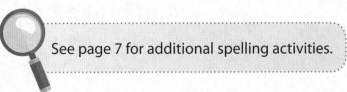

See page 7 for additional spelling activities.

Name: _____ **Date:** _____

Directions: Use a word from the Word Bank to complete each sentence.

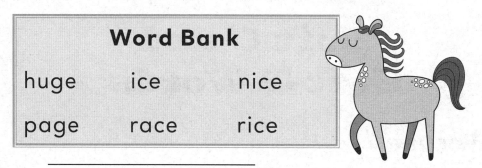

Word Bank

huge	ice	nice
page	race	rice

_____

_____

1. Don't skip a _____ when you read.

_____

_____

2. We had _____ and beans with our tacos.

_____

_____

3. Kyah is such a _____ friend to me!

_____

_____

4. Do you put _____ cubes in your water?

_____

_____

5. We watched the horses _____ around the track.

_____

_____

6. There is a _____ dent in the back of Mom's car!

Name: _____ **Date:** _____

Directions: Say the word that names each picture. Tap out the sounds in the word. Write the letter that matches each sound in a separate box. Don't forget the silent *e* at the end.

1.

_____

2.

_____

3.

_____

4.

_____

Remember that *c* and *g* each have two sounds.

Name: _____ **Date:** _____

Directions: Use a word from the Word Bank to complete each section.

Word Bank

ace	face	huge	ice
nice	pace	rage	rice

Synonym

1. front _____

2. frozen water _____

3. speed _____

Antonym

4. mean _____

5. tiny _____

6. joy _____

Write a word that fits each category.

7. bread, noodles, oatmeal, _____

8. king, ten, joker, _____

Name: _____ **Date:** _____

Directions: Look at the example. Add the same endings to each word to create two new words.

Ex. pace   paces   pacing

_____   _____

1. race   _____   _____

_____   _____

2. face   _____   _____

Directions: Look at each word. Find the related words in the Word Bank. Write the words on the correct lines.

Word Bank

iceberg   nicest

nicely   icebox

_____   _____

3. nice   _____   _____

_____   _____

4. ice   _____   _____

Inflectional Endings

Analogies

Name: _____ **Date:** _____

Directions: Use a word from the Word Bank to complete each analogy.

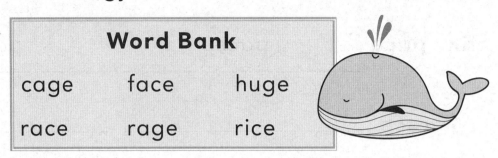

Word Bank		
cage	face	huge
race	rage	rice

1. **fish** is to **tank** as **hamster** is to _____

2. **vegetable** is to **beans** as **grain** is to _____

3. **guppy** is to **tiny** as **whale** is to _____

4. **costume** is to **body** as **mask** is to _____

5. **rink** is to **skate** as **track** is to _____

6. **happy** is to **joy** as **angry** is to _____

UNIT 15
Initial Blends with L

Focus

This week's focus is one-syllable, short vowel words that start with an *l* blend such as *bl–*, *cl–*, *fl–*, *gl–*, *pl–*, or *sl–*.

Helpful Hint

All the words on this list contain an *l* blend. *L* blends are *bl–*, *cl–*, *fl–*, *gl–*, *pl–*, and *sl–*. Always use *cl* for /k/ blends since *kl* isn't used as a blend in the English language.

- ➤ **blob**
- ➤ **clap**
- ➤ **class**
- ➤ **cliff**
- ➤ **flag**
- ➤ **glad**
- ➤ **glass**
- ➤ **plus**
- ➤ **sled**
- ➤ **slip**

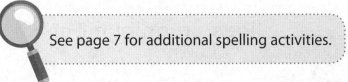

See page 7 for additional spelling activities.

Name: _____ **Date:** _____

Directions: Use a word from the Word Bank to complete each sentence.

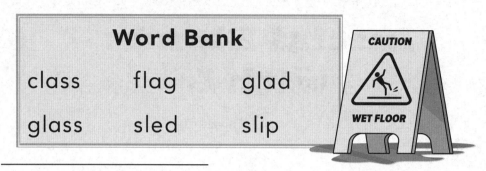

Word Bank

class	flag	glad
glass	sled	slip

1. I like to _____ down the snowy hill in my backyard.

2. The _____ of the United States is red, white, and blue.

3. The _____ vase will shatter if you drop it.

4. I'm so _____ you came!

5. Careful, don't _____ on the wet floor!

6. My _____ lines up on number 13.

Name: _____ **Date:** _____

Directions: Say the word that names each picture. Tap out the sounds in the word. Write the letter or letters that matches each sound in a separate box.

1.

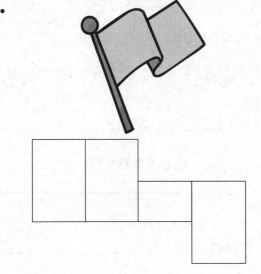

2.

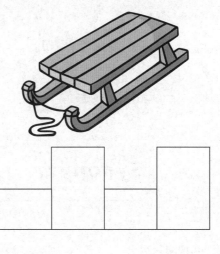

3.

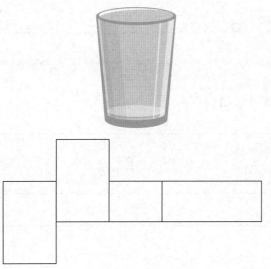

4.

Directions: Write one of the words two times.

_____   _____

_ _ _ _ _ _ _ _ _ _ _ _ _ _   _ _ _ _ _ _ _ _ _ _ _ _ _ _

Name: _____ **Date:** _____

Directions: Use words from the Word Bank to complete each section.

Word Bank		
clap	glad	glass
plus	sled	slip

Synonym	**Antonym**
1. slide _____	3. sad _____
2. applaud _____	4. minus _____

Write a word that fits each category.

5. wood, metal, paper, _____

6. skate, ski, snowshoe, _____

Name: _____ **Date:** _____

Directions: Add –*ing* to each word. Don't forget to double the consonant.

Present Tense (Now I...)	Present Tense (I am...)
clap	
hum	
slip	
sled	

Directions: Add –*ed* to each word. Don't forget to double the consonant.

Present Tense (Now I...)	Past Tense (Yesterday I...)
flip	
flag	
slap	
slam	

When adding –*ing* or –*ed* to a word that ends with a short vowel and one consonant, double the consonant.

Analogies

Name: _____ **Date:** _____

Directions: Use a word from the Word Bank to complete each analogy.

Word Bank

clap	glad	glass
plus	sled	slip

1. **fingers** is to **snap** as **hands** is to _____

2. **4 – 2** is to **minus** as **4 + 2** is to _____

3. **door** is to **wood** as **window** is to _____

4. **ice** is to **skate** as **snow** is to _____

5. **angry** is to **mad** as **happy** is to _____

6. **uneven** is to **trip** as **wet** is to _____

UNIT 16
Initial Blends with S

- scab
- skin
- smell
- snap
- spot
- stem
- still
- stop
- stuff
- swim

Focus

This week's focus is one-syllable, short vowel words that start with an *s* blend such as *sc–*, *sk–*, *sm–*, *sn–*, *sp–*, *st–*, or *sw–*.

Helpful Hint

All the words on this list contain an *s* blend. The *sc–* and *sk–* blends make the same sounds. Use *sc–* before *a*, *o*, and *u*. Use *sk–* before *e* and *i*.

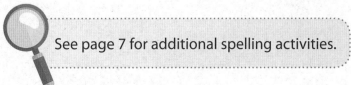

See page 7 for additional spelling activities.

Name: _____ **Date:** _____

Directions: Use a word from the Word Bank to complete each sentence.

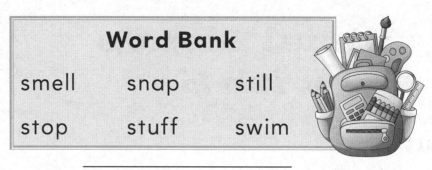

Word Bank

smell	snap	still
stop	stuff	swim

_____

1. I have too much _____ in my backpack.

_____

2. Are you _____ mad at me?

_____

3. I can't _____ my pencil box closed.

_____

4. We have to _____ at the store to buy milk.

_____

5. I like to _____ at the town pool.

_____

6. There is a bad _____ coming from the trash can.

Sentence Completions

Name: _____ **Date:** _____

Directions: Say the word that names each picture. Tap out the sounds in the word. Write the letter or letters that matches each sound in a separate box.

1.

2.

3.

4.

Directions: Write one of the words two times.

_____   _____

_ _ _ _ _ _ _ _ _   _ _ _ _ _ _ _ _ _

_____   _____

Synonyms and Antonyms

Name: _____ **Date:** _____

Directions: Use words from the Word Bank to complete each section.

Word Bank

smell	snap	spot
stem	still	stop

Synonym	**Antonym**
_____	_____
1. sniff _____	3. go _____
_____	_____
2. dot _____	4. moving _____

Write a word that fits each category.

5. leaf, petal, root, _____

6. crack, break, split, _____

Name: _____ **Date:** _____

Directions: Add *–ing* to each word. Don't forget to double the consonant.

Present Tense (Now I...)	Present Tense (I am...)
stop	
swim	
spit	
snap	

Directions: Add *–ed* to each word. Don't forget to double the consonant.

Present Tense (Now I...)	Past Tense (Yesterday I...)
scab	
stop	
snap	
spot	

Verb Tenses

Name: _____ **Date:** _____

Directions: Use a word from the Word Bank to complete each analogy.

Word Bank

smell	snap	spot
stem	stop	swim

1. **eyes** is to **see** as **nose** is to _____

2. **tree** is to **trunk** as **flower** is to _____

3. **green** is to **go** as **red** is to _____

4. **hands** is to **clap** as **fingers** is to _____

5. **zebra** is to **stripe** as **cheetah** is to _____

6. **bird** is to **fly** as **fish** is to _____

UNIT 17
Initial Blends with R

Focus

This week's focus is one-syllable, short vowel words that start with an *r* blend such as *br–*, *cr–*, *dr–*, *fr–*, *gr–*, *pr–*, or *tr–*.

Helpful Hint

All the words on this list contain an *r* blend. *R* blends are *br–*, *cr–*, *dr–*, *fr–*, *gr–*, *pr–*, and *tr–*. Be careful with *dr–* and *tr–* blends because they can sound like a /j/ (*jress/dress*) or /ch/ (*chrap/trap*).

- brag
- crab
- dress
- drop
- frog
- from
- grass
- grill
- press
- trap

See page 7 for additional spelling activities.

Name: _____ **Date:** _____

Directions: Use a word from the Word Bank to complete each sentence.

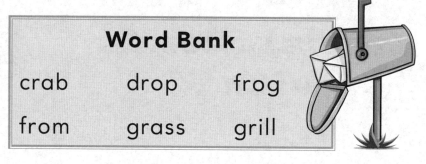

Word Bank		
crab	drop	frog
from	grass	grill

_____

1. Mom is going to _____ burgers for dinner.

_____

2. I caught a _____ in the pond near my house.

_____

3. I helped Dad plant _____ seed in the front yard.

_____

4. Use two hands so you don't _____ your lunch tray.

_____

5. I saw a _____ at the beach!

_____

6. I got a card in the mail _____ Grammy.

Name: _____ **Date:** _____

Directions: Say the word that names each picture. Tap out the sounds in the word. Write the letter or letters that matches each sound in a separate box.

1.

2.

3.

4.

Directions: Write one of the words two times.

_____   _____

_____   _____

Synonyms and Antonyms

Name: _____ **Date:** _____

Directions: Use words from the Word Bank to complete each section.

Word Bank		
crab	dress	from
grill	press	trap

Synonym	Antonym

1. gown _____   **3.** release _____

2. push _____   **4.** to _____

Write a word that fits each category.

5. cook, bake, fry, _____

6. lobster, clam, shrimp, _____

Name: _____ **Date:** _____

Directions: Add –*ing* to each word. Don't forget to double the consonant.

Present Tense (Now I...)	Present Tense (I am...)
brag	
drop	
trap	
grab	

Directions: Add –*ed* to each word. Don't forget to double the consonant.

Present Tense (Now I...)	Past Tense (Yesterday I...)
drip	
trim	
trap	
drop	

Analogies

Name: _____ **Date:** _____

Directions: Use a word from the Word Bank to complete each analogy.

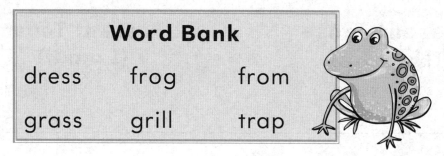

Word Bank

dress	frog	from
grass	grill	trap

1. **quack** is to **duck** as **croak** is to _____

2. **inside** is to **stove** as **outside** is to _____

3. **house** is to **carpet** as **yard** is to _____

4. **man** is to **suit** as **lady** is to _____

5. **go** is to **come** as **to** is to _____

6. **throw** is to **catch** as **release** is to _____

UNIT 18
Long A Vowel
Team *ay*

- bay
- day
- hay
- lay
- may
- pay
- ray
- say
- they
- way

Focus

This week's focus is one-syllable words that end with –ay.

Helpful Hint

All the words on this list (except *they*) use –*ay* to make a long *a* sound. When a word or syllable ends in a long *a* sound, use –*ay*. *They* is a rule breaker since the *ey* pattern usually makes a long *e* sound.

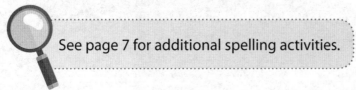

See page 7 for additional spelling activities.

Name: _____ **Date:** _____

Directions: Use a word from the Word Bank to complete each sentence.

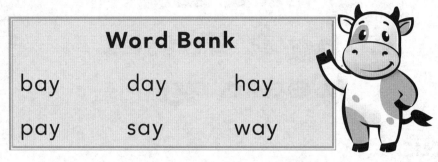

Word Bank		
bay	day	hay
pay	say	way

_____
- - - - - - - - - - - - - -

1. The cows need more _____ in the barn.

_____
- - - - - - - - - - - - - -

2. Which _____ do you want to go?

_____
- - - - - - - - - - - - - -

3. Remember to _____ please and thank you.

_____
- - - - - - - - - - - - - -

4. We need to _____ for our dinner.

_____
- - - - - - - - - - - - - -

5. I saw otters in the _____.

_____
- - - - - - - - - - - - - -

6. My favorite _____ of the week is Sunday.

Name: _____ **Date:** _____

Directions: Say the word that names each picture. Tap out the sounds in the word. Write the letter that matches each sound in a separate box.

1.

2.

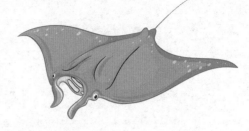

3.

4.

Directions: Write one of the words two times.

_____   _____

- - - - - - - - - - - -   - - - - - - - - - - - -

_____   _____

Synonyms and Antonyms

Name: _____ **Date:** _____

Directions: Use words from the Word Bank to complete each section.

Word Bank		
day	hay	may
pay	say	they

Synonym	Antonym
1. give	**3.** night
money	
2. speak	**4.** cannot

Write a word that fits each category.

5. he, she, we, _____

6. grass, oats, carrots, _____

Name: _____ **Date:** _____

Directions: Look at the example. Add the same endings to each word to create two new words.

Ex. lay   lays   laying

1. pay   _____   _____

          _____   _____

2. say   _____   _____

Directions: Look at each word. Find the related words in the Word Bank. Write the words on the correct lines.

Word Bank	
daylight	stingray
x-ray	daydream

3. day   _____   _____

          _____   _____

4. ray   _____   _____

Name: _____ **Date:** _____

Directions: Use a word from the Word Bank to complete each analogy.

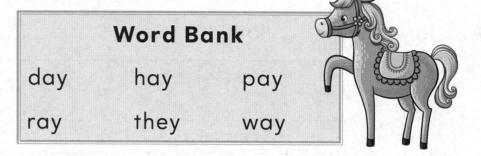

Word Bank

day	hay	pay
ray	they	way

1. **cashier** is to **ring up** as **customer** is to _____

2. **bird** is to **seeds** as **horse** is to _____

3. **lightning** is to **bolt** as **sunlight** is to _____

4. **him** is to **he** as **them** is to _____

5. **dark** is to **night** as **light** is to _____

6. **sea** is to **see** as **weigh** is to _____

UNIT 19
Long A Vowel Team *ai*

- aid
- aim
- air
- gain
- hair
- mail
- paid
- rain
- tail
- wait

Focus

This week's focus is one-syllable long *a* words that contain *ai*.

Helpful Hint

"When two vowels go walking, the first one does the talking." When two vowels are together, the first one makes its long sound and the second letter stays silent. The *ai* vowel team is only found in the middle of a syllable, never at the end.

See page 7 for additional spelling activities.

Sentence Completions

Name: _____ **Date:** _____

Directions: Use a word from the Word Bank to complete each sentence.

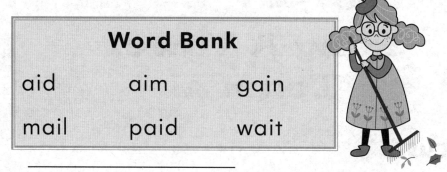

Word Bank		
aid	aim	gain
mail	paid	wait

1. We had to _____ in line for our movie tickets.

2. Dad checked the first _____ kit.

3. Try to _____ for the catcher's mitt when you pitch.

4. Grandpa _____ me $10 to rake his yard!

5. The baby will _____ ten pounds and grow five inches.

6. Please check the _____ to see if my package came.

Name: _____ **Date:** _____

Directions: Say the word that names each picture. Tap out the sounds in the word. Write the letter or letters that matches each sound in a separate box.

1.

2.

3.

4.

Directions: Write one of the words two times.

_____   _____

- - - - - - - - - - - - - - - -   - - - - - - - - - - - - - - - -

_____   _____

Synonyms and Antonyms

Name: _____ **Date:** _____

Directions: Use words from the Word Bank to complete each section.

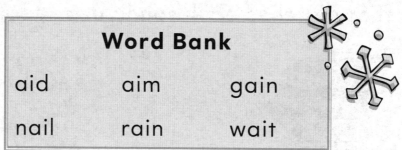

Word Bank

aid	aim	gain
nail	rain	wait

Synonym	Antonym
1. help _____	**3.** rush _____
2. point at _____	**4.** lose _____

Write a word that fits each category.

5. snow, sleet, hail, _____

6. tack, push pin, screw, _____

Name: _____ **Date:** _____

Directions: Look at the examples. Add the same endings to each word to create two new words.

Ex. sail   sails   sailing
        _____   _____
- -
1. mail   _____   _____

Ex. gain   gains   gaining
        _____   _____
- -
2. rain   _____   _____

Directions: Look at each word. Find the related words in the Word Bank. Write the words on the correct lines.

Word Bank	
fingernail	hairspray
hairbrush	toenail

        _____   _____
- -
3. nail   _____   _____

        _____   _____
- -
4. hair   _____   _____

Analogies

Name: _____ **Date:** _____

Directions: Use a word from the Word Bank to complete each analogy.

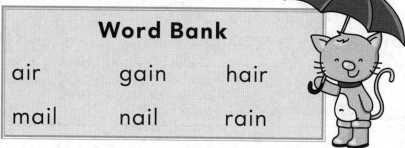

Word Bank		
air	gain	hair
mail	nail	rain

1. **dog** is to **fur** as **person** is to _____

2. **pencil** is to **pen** as **screw** is to _____

3. **shrink** is to **grow** as **lose** is to _____

4. **heart** is to **blood** as **lungs** is to _____

5. **winter** is to **snow** as **spring** is to _____

6. **market** is to **food** as **post office** is to _____

UNIT 20
Long E Vowel Team ea

- beak
- each
- eat
- hear
- leaf
- mean
- read
- real
- seal
- teach

Focus

This week's focus is one-syllable long *e* words that contain *ea*.

Helpful Hint

The *ea* vowel team can be found at the beginning, middle, or end of a word or syllable (*eat*, *leaf*, *tea*).

See page 7 for additional spelling activities.

Name: _____ **Date:** _____

Directions: Use a word from the Word Bank to complete each sentence.

Word Bank

beak	each	hear
read	seal	teach

_____

1. Mom lets me _____ before bed.

_____

2. A hummingbird uses its long _____ to get nectar from flowers.

_____

3. Mrs. Shah is going to _____ us how to add big numbers.

_____

4. You may _____ have one candy bar.

_____

5. The _____ balanced a ball on his nose.

_____

6. Please talk louder. I can't _____ what you're saying.

Name: _____ **Date:** _____

Directions: Say the word that names each picture. Tap out the sounds in the word. Write the letter or letters that matches each sound in a separate box.

1.

2.

3.

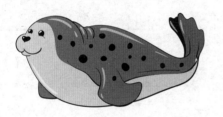

4.

Directions: Write one of the words two times.

_____

_ _ _ _ _ _ _ _ _ _ _ _ _ _   _ _ _ _ _ _ _ _ _ _ _ _ _ _

_____

Name: _____ **Date:** _____

Directions: Use words from the Word Bank to complete each section.

Word Bank

each	hear	leaf
real	seal	teach

Synonym	**Antonym**
1. listen _____	3. learn _____
	_____
2. per person _____	4. fake _____

Write a word that fits each category.

5. trunk, roots, branch, _____

6. walrus, dolphin, whale, _____

28629—180 Days of Spelling and Word Study

Verb Tenses

Name: _____ **Date:** _____

Directions: Add –ed to each word.

Present Tense (Now I...)	Past Tense (Yesterday I...)
leap	
heal	
heat	
lean	

Directions: Write the past tense of each word.

Present Tense (Now I...)	Past Tense (Yesterday I...)
eat	
hear	
lead	
teach	

Some words don't follow the –ed rule. They look and sound like a whole new word when they change to the past tense.

Analogies

Name: _____ **Date:** _____

Directions: Use a word from the Word Bank to complete each analogy.

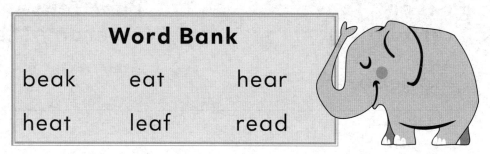

Word Bank

beak	eat	hear
heat	leaf	read

1. **flower** is to **petal** as **stem** is to _____

2. **elephant** is to **trunk** as **bird** is to _____

3. **eyes** is to **see** as **ears** is to _____

4. **water** is to **drink** as **food** is to _____

5. **fan** is to **cool** as **fireplace** is to _____

6. **TV** is to **watch** as **book** is to _____

UNIT 21
Long E Vowel Team ee

Focus

This week's focus is one-syllable long *e* words that contain *ee*.

Helpful Hint

The *ee* vowel team makes a long *e* sound, just like *ea*. It can also be found at the beginning, middle, or end of a word or syllable (*eel*, *feed*, *see*). There is no trick or rule to know which pattern to use, so it's best to try *ee* and *ea* when writing a word and see which one "looks" right.

➤ **been**
➤ **feed**
➤ **feel**
➤ **keep**
➤ **meet**
➤ **need**
➤ **queen**
➤ **seem**
➤ **week**
➤ **wheel**

See page 7 for additional spelling activities.

Name: _____ **Date:** _____

Directions: Use a word from the Word Bank to complete each sentence.

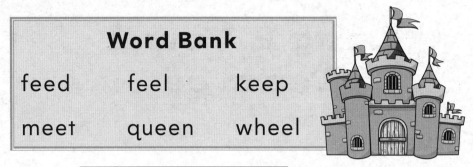

Word Bank

feed	feel	keep
meet	queen	wheel

_____
_ _ _ _ _ _ _ _ _ _ _

1. Don't forget to _____ the dog before school!

_____
_ _ _ _ _ _ _ _ _ _ _

2. The _____ on the my bike is squeaky.

_____
_ _ _ _ _ _ _ _ _ _ _

3. Will you _____ me at the park?

_____
_ _ _ _ _ _ _ _ _ _ _

4. If you don't _____ well, you should go see the nurse.

_____
_ _ _ _ _ _ _ _ _ _ _

5. The king and _____ live in a castle.

_____
_ _ _ _ _ _ _ _ _ _ _

6. I _____ an extra pair of socks in my backpack.

Name: _____ Date: _____

Directions: Use words from the Word Bank to complete each section.

Word Bank		
feed	feel	keep
queen	week	wheel

Synonym	Antonym
1. touch _____	3. king _____
2. give food _____	4. give away _____

Write a word that fits each category.

5. day, month, year, _____

6. pedal, seat, chain, _____

Verb Tenses

Name: _____ **Date:** _____

Directions: Add –*ed* to each word.

Present Tense (Now I...)	Past Tense (Yesterday I...)
peek	
peel	
need	
wheel	

Directions: Write the past tense of each word.

Present Tense (Now I...)	Past Tense (Yesterday I...)
keep	
feed	
meet	
feel	

Name: _____ **Date:** _____

Directions: Study each example. Write the same kind of sentence using each word.

QUESTION **Ex.** *meet*: Did you *meet* your teacher?

_____

1. *wheel*: _____

_____

_____

2. *queen*: _____

_____

_____

STATEMENT **Ex.** *feet*: My *feet* are big.

_____

3. *week*: _____

_____

_____

4. *feed*: _____

_____

_____

Sentence Types

Analogies

Name: _____ **Date:** _____

Directions: Use a word from the Word Bank to complete each analogy.

Word Bank		
feel	keep	meet
queen	week	wheel

1. **365 days** is to **year** as **7 days** is to _____

2. **car** is to **tire** as **bike** is to _____

3. **prince** is to **princess** as **king** is to _____

4. **eyes** is to **see** as **fingers** is to _____

5. **sea** is to **see** as **meat** is to _____

6. **wept** is to **weep** as **kept** is to _____

UNIT 22
Long O Vowel Team oa

Focus

This week's focus is one-syllable long *o* words that contain *oa*.

Helpful Hint

The *oa* vowel team makes a long *o* sound. It is only found at the beginning or middle of a word or syllable (*oat*, *road*). It is never found at the end of a word.

- ➤ **boat**
- ➤ **coat**
- ➤ **foam**
- ➤ **goal**
- ➤ **goat**
- ➤ **load**
- ➤ **moan**
- ➤ **road**
- ➤ **soak**
- ➤ **soap**

See page 7 for additional spelling activities.

Name: _____ **Date:** _____

Directions: Use a word from the Word Bank to complete each sentence.

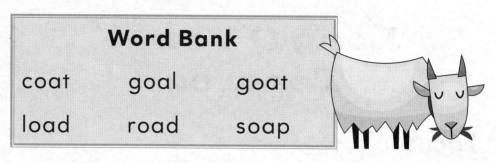

Word Bank		
coat	goal	goat
load	road	soap

_____
- - - - - - - - - - - - - - -

1. We need to _____ the truck with boxes.

_____
- - - - - - - - - - - - - - -

2. Use _____ and warm water when you wash your hands.

_____
- - - - - - - - - - - - - - -

3. Abby scored a _____ during the first half of the game.

_____
- - - - - - - - - - - - - - -

4. Put a _____ on. It's cold outside!

_____
- - - - - - - - - - - - - - -

5. The _____ on my uncle's farm will eat anything!

_____
- - - - - - - - - - - - - - -

6. The _____ in front of my house was being worked on.

28629—180 Days of Spelling and Word Study   © *Shell Education*

Sentence Completions

Name: _____ **Date:** _____

Directions: Use words from the Word Bank to complete each section.

Word Bank

coat	goal	load
moan	road	soap

Synonym   **Antonym**

_____   _____

1. jacket _____   **3.** giggle _____

_____   _____

2. street _____   **4.** unload _____

Write a word that fits each category.

_____

5. run, basket, touchdown, _____

_____

6. shampoo, conditioner, bath gel, _____

Inflectional Endings

Name: _____ **Date:** _____

Directions: Look at the examples. Add the same endings to each word to create two new words.

Ex. loan   loans   loaning

_____   _____

1. moan _____   _____

Ex. roam   roams   roaming

_____   _____

2. foam _____   _____

Directions: Look at each word. Find the related words in the Word Bank. Write the words on the correct lines.

Word Bank	
railroad	sailboat
tugboat	roadwork

_____   _____

3. road _____   _____

_____   _____

4. boat _____   _____

Name: _____ **Date:** _____

Directions: Study each example. Write the same kind of sentence using each word.

QUESTION **Ex.** *loan:* Can you *loan* me a dollar?

_____

1. *soap:* _____

_____

_____

_____

2. *load:* _____

_____

_____

_____

STATEMENT **Ex.** *soak:* I'm going to *soak* in the tub.

_____

3. *boat:* _____

_____

_____

_____

4. *goat:* _____

_____

_____

_____

Name: _____ Date: _____

Directions: Use a word from the Word Bank to complete each analogy.

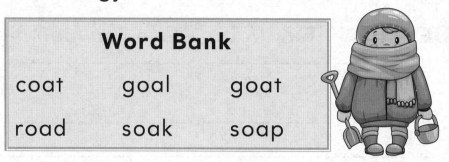

Word Bank		
coat	goal	goat
road	soak	soap

1. **hot** is to **T-shirt** as **cold** is to _____

   _____

2. **hair** is to **shampoo** as **body** is to _____

   _____

3. **shower** is to **rinse** as **tub** is to _____

   _____

4. **bike** is to **path** as **car** is to _____

   _____

5. **zoo** is to **monkey** as **farm** is to _____

   _____

6. **baseball** is to **run** as **soccer** is to _____

UNIT 23
Long O Vowel Teams oe and ow

Focus

This week's focus is one-syllable long *o* words that contain *oe* or *ow*.

Helpful Hint

Both *oe* and *ow* make a long *o* sound. Unlike *oa*, they can be found at the end of a syllable or word. A second /*ow*/ sound will be explored in a later unit.

➤ bow
➤ foe
➤ grow
➤ low
➤ mow
➤ row
➤ show
➤ snow
➤ toe
➤ tow

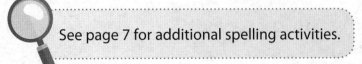
See page 7 for additional spelling activities.

Name: _____ **Date:** _____

Directions: Use a word from the Word Bank to complete each sentence.

Word Bank

bow	grow	low
mow	row	tow

_____

1. I like to _____ vegetables in the garden.

_____

2. The gift had a big red _____ on top.

_____

3. My little brother pretends to _____ the lawn.

_____

4. Esteban called a _____ truck when his car broke down.

_____

5. Mom and Dad sat in the front _____ during my concert.

_____

6. Dad keeps snacks on a _____ shelf so we can reach them.

28629—180 Days of Spelling and Word Study

Sentence Completions

Name: _____ **Date:** _____

Directions: Say the word that names each picture. Tap out the sounds in the word. Write the letter or letters that matches each sound in a separate box.

1.

2.

3.

4.

Directions: Write one of the words two times.

_____   _____

- - - - - - - - - - - - - - - - - -   - - - - - - - - - - - - - - - - - -

_____   _____

Synonyms and Antonyms

Name: _____ **Date:** _____

Directions: Use words from the Word Bank to complete each section.

Word Bank

| foe | low | row |
| show | snow | toe |

Synonym	**Antonym**
_____	_____
1. paddle _____	3. friend _____
2. display _____	4. high _____

Write a word that fits each category.

_____

5. rain, hail, sleet, _____

6. finger, nose, ear, _____

Name: _____ **Date:** _____

Directions: Homophones sound the same but have different spellings and meanings. Write the correct homophone on each line.

_____

_ _ _ _ _ _ _

1. I am _____ hungry!
   (sew/so)

_ _ _ _ _ _ _

2. Do you _____ how to play checkers?
   (know/no)

_____

_ _ _ _ _ _ _

3. I helped Mom roll out the cookie _____ .
   (doe/dough)

_____

_ _ _ _ _ _ _

4. I asked Dad for a snack but he said _____ .
   (know/no)

_____

_ _ _ _ _ _ _

5. My neighbor is going to _____ the
   patches on my pants.   (sew/so)

_____

_ _ _ _ _ _ _

6. My big _____ is sticking out of my sock.
   (toe/tow)

Analogies

Name: _____ **Date:** _____

Directions: Use a word from the Word Bank to complete each analogy.

Word Bank		
bow	foe	low
mow	toe	tow

1. **up** is to **down** as **high** is to _____

2. **hair** is to **cut** as **lawn** is to _____

3. **rope** is to **knot** as **ribbon** is to _____

4. **hand** is to **finger** as **foot** is to _____

5. **friend** is to **ally** as **enemy** is to _____

6. **no** is to **know** as **toe** is to _____

UNIT 24

Long *I* Patterns
ie and *y*

- ➤ cry
- ➤ die
- ➤ dry
- ➤ fly
- ➤ lie
- ➤ pie
- ➤ sky
- ➤ tie
- ➤ try
- ➤ why

Focus

This week's focus is one-syllable long *i* words that contain *ie* or *y*.

Helpful Hint

Y always has a long *i* sound when it appears after a consonant at the end of a one-syllable word (*by, my, fry*). *Y* has a long *e* sound at the end of two-syllable words (*ba·by, la·dy*) unless the second syllable is stressed (*re·ply, de·ny*).

See page 7 for additional spelling activities.

Name: _____ **Date:** _____

Directions: Use a word from the Word Bank to complete each sentence.

Word Bank		
dry	lie	pie
sky	tie	try

_____

1. The _____ looked beautiful at sunset tonight.

_____

2. Apple _____ is my favorite dessert!

_____

3. I used a towel to _____ the dishes.

_____

4. I want you to _____ one bite and see if you like it.

_____

5. You should never _____ to your parents.

_____

6. The teddy bear had a _____ around its neck.

Name: _____ **Date:** _____

Directions: Say the word that names each picture. Tap out the sounds in the word. Write the letter or letters that matches each sound in a separate box.

1.

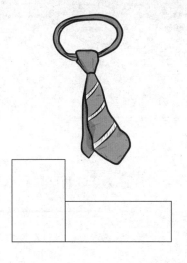

2.

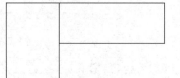

3.

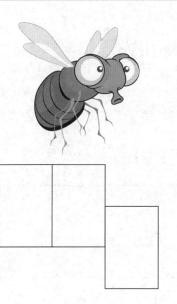

4.

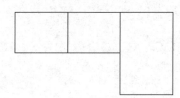

Directions: Write one of the words two times.

_____   _____

_____   _____

Name: _____ Date: _____

Directions: Use words from the Word Bank to complete each section.

Word Bank		
cry	dry	pie
tie	try	why

Synonym	Antonym
1. attempt _____	3. wet _____
	_____
2. make a knot _____	4. laugh _____

Write a word that fits each category.

5. cake, cookies, ice cream, _____

6. who, what, when, _____

Name: _____ **Date:** _____

Directions: Look at the example. Add the same endings to each word to create two new words.

Ex. tie   ties   tying

1. die _____ _____

2. lie _____ _____

Directions: Look at each word. Find the related words in the Word Bank. Write the words on the correct lines.

Word Bank	
flies	dryer
dried	butterfly

3. dry _____ _____

4. fly _____ _____

Name: _____ **Date:** _____

Directions: Use a word from the Word Bank to complete each analogy.

Word Bank

cry	dry	fly
pie	sky	tie

1. **frosting** is to **cake** as **crust** is to _____

2. **green** is to **grass** as **blue** is to _____

3. **dog** is to **bark** as **baby** is to _____

4. **sponge** is to **clean** as **towel** is to _____

5. **waist** is to **belt** as **neck** is to _____

6. **fish** is to **swim** as **bird** is to _____

UNIT 25

Long I Pattern igh

Focus

This week's focus is one-syllable long *i* words that contain *igh*.

Helpful Hint

All the words on this list contain *igh*. The *igh* pattern always has a long *i* sound unless it follows an *e* (*weigh*, *neighbor*).

> See page 7 for additional spelling activities.

➤ fight

➤ high

➤ light

➤ might

➤ night

➤ right

➤ sigh

➤ sight

➤ thigh

➤ tight

Name: _____ **Date:** _____

Directions: Use a word from the Word Bank to complete each sentence.

Sentence Completions

Word Bank		
fight	high	light
might	right	sigh

1. Mom sends us to our room when we _____ with each other.

2. I _____ be a doctor when I grow up.

3. Dad keeps all his tools on a _____ shelf so Leila can't reach them.

4. Don't forget to turn off the _____!

5. I catch with my _____ hand.

6. I can hear you _____ when you get frustrated.

Name: _____ **Date:** _____

Directions: Use words from the Word Bank to complete each section.

Word Bank		
fight	high	light
right	sight	thigh

Synonym   **Antonym**

1. argue _____   3. low _____

2. correct _____   4. dark _____

 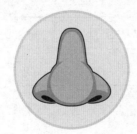  

Write a word that fits each category.

5. shin, calf, knee, _____

6. taste, smell, hearing, _____

Name: _____ **Date:** _____

Directions: Homophones sound the same but have different spellings and meanings. Write the correct homophone on each line.

Homophones

_____

1. I say _____ to my friends when I see them. **(hi/high)**

_____

2. I woke up during the storm last _____ . **(knight/night)**

_____

3. We walked _____ the river today. **(by/bye)**

_____

4. The cans are too _____ . I can't reach them. **(hi/high)**

_____

5. I learned how to _____ my name when I was four. **(right/write)**

_____

6. Eddie waved _____ from the backseat of the car. **(by/bye)**

Name: _____ **Date:** _____

Directions: Answer each question in a complete sentence. Use the bold word in each answer.

1. Why do children's clothes get **tight**?

_____

_ _ _ _ _ _ _ _ _ _ _ _ _ _ _ _ _

_____

_ _ _ _ _ _ _ _ _ _ _ _ _ _ _ _ _

_____

2. Why do some people sleep with a **light** on?

_____

_ _ _ _ _ _ _ _ _ _ _ _ _ _ _ _ _

_____

_ _ _ _ _ _ _ _ _ _ _ _ _ _ _ _ _

_____

3. Why do people **sigh**?

_____

_ _ _ _ _ _ _ _ _ _ _ _ _ _ _ _ _

_____

_ _ _ _ _ _ _ _ _ _ _ _ _ _ _ _ _

_____

Name: _____ **Date:** _____

Directions: Use a word from the Word Bank to complete each analogy.

Word Bank

fight	high	light
night	right	sight

1. **light** is to **day** as **dark** is to _____

2. **furnace** is to **heat** as **lamp** is to _____

3. **police** is to **protect** as **soldier** is to _____

4. **down** is to **low** as **up** is to _____

5. **ears** is to **hearing** as **eyes** is to _____

6. **bad** is to **good** as **wrong** is to _____

UNIT 26
Long U Pattern oo

Focus

This week's focus is one-syllable long *u* words that contain *oo*.

Helpful Hint

The *oo* pattern makes two sounds. It can sound like long *u* (*soon*) or take on a short vowel sound (*book*). All the *oo* words on this list have a long *u* sound.

- cool
- food
- loop
- mood
- moon
- noon
- pool
- roof
- room
- soon

See page 7 for additional spelling activities.

Sentence Completions

Name: _____ **Date:** _____

Directions: Use a word from the Word Bank to complete each sentence.

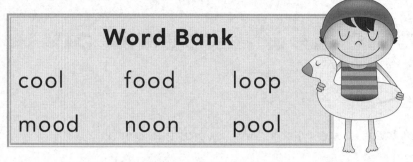

Word Bank

cool	food	loop
mood	noon	pool

_____
- - - - - - - - -

1. I was in a bad _____ after school today.

_____
- - - - - - - - -

2. Let the cookies _____ after you take them out of the oven.

_____
- - - - - - - - -

3. We swam in my neighbor's _____ for three hours yesterday.

_____
- - - - - - - - -

4. I like to make _____ for my family.

_____
- - - - - - - - -

5. Is it almost _____? I'm ready for lunch!

_____
- - - - - - - - -

6. Raj showed me how to make a _____ when I tie my shoes.

Name: _____ **Date:** _____

Directions: Use words from the Word Bank to complete each section.

Word Bank		
cool	moon	noon
pool	roof	soon

Synonym	Antonym
_____	_____
1. housetop _____	3. warm _____
	_____
2. in a little while _____	4. midnight _____

Write a word that fits each category.

_____

5. lake, pond, bathtub, _____

_____

6. sun, star, planet, _____

Name: _____ **Date:** _____

Directions: Look at the examples. Add the same endings to each word to create two new words.

Ex. fool   fools   fooling
_____   _____

1. cool _____   _____

Ex. boom   booms   booming
_____   _____

2. room _____   _____

Directions: Look at each word. Find the related words in the Word Bank. Write the words on the correct lines.

Word Bank

moonlight   rooftop

sunroof   moons

3. moon _____   _____

4. roof _____   _____

Name: _____ **Date:** _____

Directions: Answer each question in a complete sentence. Use the bold word in each answer.

1. How do you stay safe at the **pool**?

_____

_____

_____

_____

2. What do you do to stay **cool**?

_____

_____

_____

_____

3. What is your favorite **food**?

_____

_____

_____

_____

Turn the Question Around

Name: _____ **Date:** _____

Directions: Use a word from the Word Bank to complete each analogy.

Analogies

Word Bank

| cool | food | moon |
| noon | pool | tool |

1. **dark** is to **midnight** as **light** is to _____

2. **oven** is to **heat** as **refrigerator** is to _____

3. **sip** is to **beverage** as **eat** is to _____

4. **day** is to **sun** as **night** is to _____

5. **run** is to **field** as **swim** is to _____

6. **teacher** is to **pencil** as **worker** is to _____

UNIT 27

Long U Vowel Teams ue and ew

Focus

This week's focus is one-syllable long *u* words that contain *ue* or *ew*.

Helpful Hint

Both *ue* and *ew* make the same long *u* sound. They are usually found at the end of a syllable or word (*blue, jewel*).

- ➤ blue
- ➤ chew
- ➤ clue
- ➤ dew
- ➤ due
- ➤ few
- ➤ flew
- ➤ glue
- ➤ new
- ➤ stew

See page 7 for additional spelling activities.

Sentence Completions

Name: _____ **Date:** _____

Directions: Use a word from the Word Bank to complete each sentence.

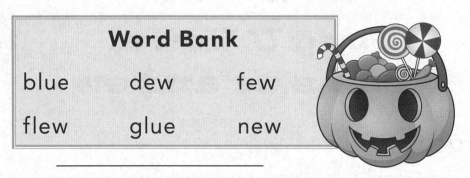

Word Bank		
blue	dew	few
flew	glue	new

_____

- - - - - - - -

1. I only have a _____ pieces of Halloween candy left.

_____

- - - - - - -

2. I love my _____ backpack!

_____

- - - - - - -

3. The bird _____ away when we went out for recess.

_____

- - - - - - -

4. Our jerseys are red and _____.

_____

- - - - - - -

5. Can you _____ the picture frame back together?

_____

- - - - - - -

6. The grass was wet with _____ this morning.

Name: _____ **Date:** _____

Directions: Use words from the Word Bank to complete each section.

Word Bank		
blue	dew	few
glue	new	stew

Synonym	Antonym
1. paste _____	3. many _____
2. water droplets _____	4. old _____

Write a word that fits each category.

5. red, green, yellow, _____

6. soup, broth, chowder, _____

Homophones

Name: _____ **Date:** _____

Directions: Homophones sound the same but have different spellings and meanings. Write the correct homophone on each line.

1. Let's finish the project. It's _____ tomorrow.
   (dew/do/due)

2. I am _____ tired to stay awake.
   (to/too/two)

3. The leaves were wet with _____ .
   (dew/do/due)

4. I can carry _____ gallons of milk at the same time.
   (to/too/two)

5. Did your dad drive you _____ school?
   (to/too/two)

6. I don't need help. I can _____ it all by myself.
   (dew/do/due)

Name: _____ **Date:** _____

Directions: Look at the examples. Add the same endings to each word to create new words.

Ex. stew   stews   stewing

          _____   _____
          -
1. chew   _____   _____

Ex. sue   sues   suing

          _____   _____
          -
2. glue   _____   _____

Directions: Look at each word. Find the related words in the Word Bank. Write the words on the correct lines.

Word Bank	
newer	bluebird
blueberry	newest

          _____   _____
          -
3. blue   _____   _____

          _____   _____
          -
4. new   _____   _____

Name: _____ **Date:** _____

Directions: Use a word from the Word Bank to complete each analogy.

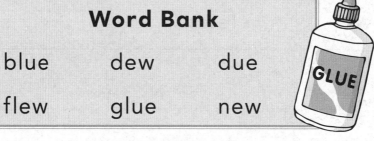

Word Bank

blue	dew	due
flew	glue	new

1. **wood** is to **nails** as **paper** is to _____

2. **grass** is to **green** as **sky** is to _____

3. **swim** is to **swam** as **fly** is to _____

4. **dirty** is to **clean** as **old** is to _____

5. **winter** is to **frost** as **summer** is to _____

6. **no** is to **know** as **dew** is to _____

UNIT 28
Words with Schwa

Focus

This week's focus is one-syllable words that use *oo* or *u* to make the schwa sound.

Helpful Hint

All the words on this list contain a schwa sound. The schwa is a lazy vowel sound that is pronounced /*uh*/. It's considered lazy because people barely have to open their mouths to pronounce it. Schwa can be represented by any vowel. On this list, it is represented by *oo* and *u*.

- ➤ **book**
- ➤ **foot**
- ➤ **full**
- ➤ **good**
- ➤ **look**
- ➤ **pull**
- ➤ **push**
- ➤ **put**
- ➤ **took**
- ➤ **wood**

See page 7 for additional spelling activities.

Name: _____ **Date:** _____

Directions: Use a word from the Word Bank to complete each sentence.

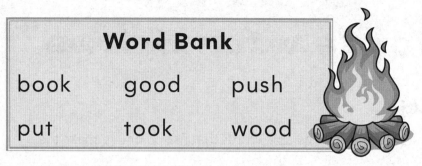

Word Bank		
book	good	push
put	took	wood

_____

1. Will you _____ me on the swing?

_____

2. Mom _____ us out for ice cream yesterday.

_____

3. My big sister reads me a _____ before bed every night.

_____

4. Please _____ your dishes in the sink.

_____

5. Dad said I did a _____ job cleaning my room.

_____

6. We need to add more _____ to the campfire.

Name: _____ **Date:** _____

Directions: Use words from the Word Bank to complete each section.

Word Bank		
foot	full	good
look	pull	wood

Synonym	Antonym
1. yank _____	3. hungry _____
2. lumber _____	4. bad _____

Write a word that fits each category.

5. peek, see, glance, _____

6. arm, leg, hand, _____

Verb Tenses

Name: _____ **Date:** _____

Directions: Add *–ed* to each word.

Present Tense (Now I...)	Past Tense (Yesterday I...)
look	
cook	
pull	
push	

Directions: Write the past tense of each word.

Present Tense (Now I...)	Past Tense (Yesterday I...)
take	
shake	
stand	
fly	

Name: _____ **Date:** _____

Directions: Answer each question in a complete sentence. Use the bold word in each answer.

1. Why do people **look** in the mirror?

_____

_____

- -

_____

2. What's your favorite **book**?

_____

- -

_____

_____

3. Why do people **pull** weeds out of their gardens?

_____

- -

_____

_____

Turn the Question Around

Analogies

Name: _____ **Date:** _____

Directions: Use a word from the Word Bank to complete each analogy.

Word Bank		
book	foot	look
pull	took	wood

1. **mitten** is to **hand** as **sock** is to _____

2. **car** is to **gas** as **fireplace** is to _____

3. **give** is to **take** as **push** is to _____

4. **watch** is to **movie** as **read** is to _____

5. **give** is to **gave** as **take** is to _____

6. **hear** is to **listen** as **see** is to _____

UNIT 29

ou and ow Diphthongs

➤ about

➤ couch

➤ down

➤ gown

➤ how

➤ loud

➤ mouth

➤ now

➤ out

➤ town

Focus

This week's focus is one-syllable words that contain *ou* or *ow*.

Helpful Hint

The diphthong *ou* (*out*, *loud*) can be found at the beginning or middle of many words, but never at the end. The diphthong *ow* is mostly used at the end of a word (*how*, *cow*) unless it comes before *n* (*brown*), *d* (*crowd*), or *l* (*howl*).

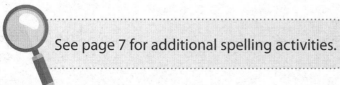

See page 7 for additional spelling activities.

Name: _____ **Date:** _____

Directions: Use a word from the Word Bank to complete each sentence.

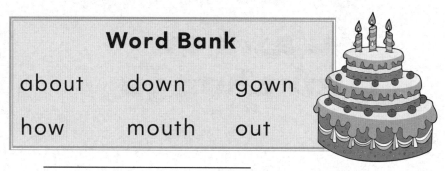

Word Bank		
about	down	gown
how	mouth	out

_____

1. The queen's _____ was beautiful.

_____

2. I have to take the garbage _____ every Monday.

_____

3. My teacher read a book _____ the Pilgrims.

_____

4. Please close your _____ when you're chewing.

_____

5. I want to learn _____ to make a cake.

_____

6. My baseball rolled _____ the street and into a bush.

Sentence Completions

Name: _____ **Date:** _____

Directions: Say the word that names each picture. Tap out the sounds in the word. Write the letter or letters that matches each sound in a separate box.

1.

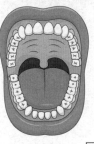

2.

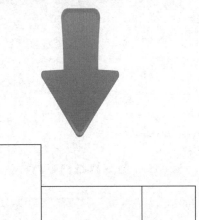

3.

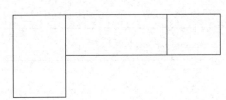

4.

Directions: Write one of the words two times.

_____   _____

- - - - - - - - - - - - - - - -   - - - - - - - - - - - - - - - -

_____   _____

Name: _____ **Date:** _____

Directions: Use words from the Word Bank to complete each section.

Synonyms and Antonyms

Word Bank		
couch	how	loud
mouth	out	town

Synonym	Antonym
1. village _____	3. in _____
2. sofa _____	4. quiet _____

Write a word that fits each category.

5. when, where, why, _____

6. nose, cheeks, chin, _____

Name: _____ **Date:** _____

Directions: To make a word mean *more than one*, add an –s to the end of the word. It becomes a plural. Write each word with an –s on the end to show it means more than one. If a word ends with –ch, –sh, –x, or –s, make it plural by adding –es.

Singular Noun (One)	Plural Noun (More Than One)
town	
mouth	
couch	
gown	
noun	
cow	
cloud	
pouch	

Analogies

Name: _____ **Date:** _____

Directions: Use a word from the Word Bank to complete each analogy.

Word Bank

couch	down	gown
loud	mouth	town

1. **smell** is to **nose** as **eat** is to _____

2. **ladder** is to **up** as **slide** is to _____

3. **big** is to **city** as **small** is to _____

4. **library** is to **quiet** as **recess** is to _____

5. **groom** is to **suit** as **bride** is to _____

6. **small** is to **chair** as **big** is to _____

UNIT 30

oi and oy Diphthongs

➤ boil
➤ boy
➤ coil
➤ coin
➤ foil
➤ join
➤ joy
➤ oil
➤ soil
➤ toy

Focus

This week's focus is one-syllable words that contain *oi* or *oy*.

Helpful Hint

All the words on this list have an */oy/* sound. The */oy/* is spelled with *oi* or *oy*. Notice that *oi* always appears at the beginning or middle of a syllable (*oil, join*), while *oy* always appears at the end of a word or syllable (*foy·er, joy*).

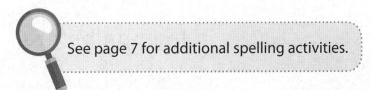

See page 7 for additional spelling activities.

Sentence Completions

Name: _____ **Date:** _____

Directions: Use a word from the Word Bank to complete each sentence.

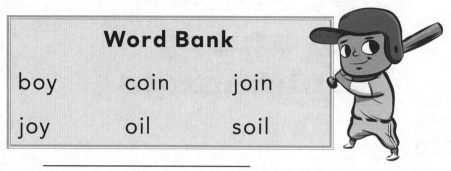

Word Bank		
boy	coin	join
joy	oil	soil

_____

_ _ _ _ _ _ _ _ _ _

1. I'm going to _____ a baseball team this year.

_____

_ _ _ _ _ _ _ _ _ _

2. Only one other _____ waits at my bus stop.

_____

_ _ _ _ _ _ _ _ _ _

3. The _____ in the planter is dry.

_____

_ _ _ _ _ _ _ _ _ _

4. This puppy brings so much _____ to my family!

_____

_ _ _ _ _ _ _ _ _ _

5. My favorite _____ is my state quarter.

_____

_ _ _ _ _ _ _ _ _ _

6. Rose put _____ in the pan before making the pancakes.

Name: _____ **Date:** _____

Directions: Use words from the Word Bank to complete each section.

Word Bank		
coin	foil	join
joy	oil	soil

Synonym	Antonym
_____	_____
1. dirt _____	3. quit _____
_____	_____
2. grease _____	4. sorrow _____

Write a word that fits each category.

_____

5. check, credit card, dollar bill, _____

_____

6. plastic wrap, baggie, container, _____

Name: _____ **Date:** _____

Directions: Look at the examples. Add the same endings to each word to create new words.

Ex. toil   toils   toiling
_____   _____

1. boil   _____   _____

Ex. coin   coins   coining
_____   _____

2. join   _____   _____

Directions: Look at each word. Find the related words in the Word Bank. Write the words on the correct lines.

Word Bank	
oils	joyful
enjoy	oiled

_____   _____

3. joy   _____   _____

_____   _____

4. oil   _____   _____

Name: _____ **Date:** _____

Directions: Answer each question in a complete sentence. Use the bold word in each answer.

1. What is a **coin**?

_____

- -

_____

- -

_____

2. What is your favorite **toy**?

_____

- -

_____

- -

_____

3. Which club or team would you like to **join**?

_____

- -

_____

- -

_____

Turn the Question Around

Analogies

Name: _____ **Date:** _____

Directions: Use a word from the Word Bank to complete each analogy.

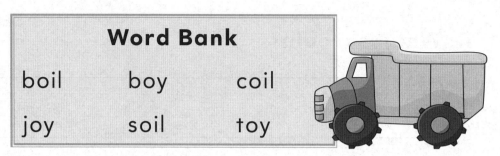

Word Bank		
boil	boy	coil
joy	soil	toy

1. **fish** is to **water** as **worm** is to _____

2. **she** is to **girl** as **he** is to _____

3. **cold** is to **freeze** as **hot** is to _____

4. **sadness** is to **sad** as **joyful** is to _____

5. **pull rope** is to **tug** as **wrap rope** is to _____

6. **dad's truck** is to **real** as **kid's truck** is to _____

UNIT 31
Words with /aw/ Sound

Focus

This week's focus is one-syllable words that use *al*, *aw*, or *o* to make the /*aw*/ sound.

Helpful Hint

All the words on this list have an /*aw*/ sound. The /*aw*/ sound can be made with *aw*, *al*, or *o*.

- ball
- fall
- jaw
- lawn
- loss
- saw
- talk
- tall
- toss
- walk

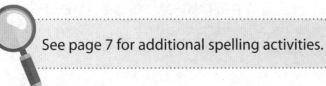
See page 7 for additional spelling activities.

Name: _____ **Date:** _____

Directions: Use a word from the Word Bank to complete each sentence.

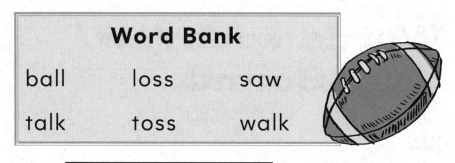

Word Bank

ball	loss	saw
talk	toss	walk

_____

1. You shouldn't _____ during a movie.

_____

2. Camila chose a bouncy _____ from the prize box.

_____

3. Let's _____ the ball around for a while before the game starts.

_____

4. I _____ to school every day.

_____

5. The football team was sad after their _____ .

_____

6. We _____ that movie at the theater on Friday.

Name: _____ **Date:** _____

Directions: Use words from the Word Bank to complete each section.

Word Bank		
fall	lawn	loss
talk	tall	toss

Synonym	Antonym
_____	_____
1. grass _____	**3.** win _____
	_____
2. throw _____	**4.** short _____

Write a word that fits each category.

_____

5. winter, summer, spring, _____

_____

6. speak, say, chat, _____

Inflectional Endings

Name: _____ **Date:** _____

Directions: Look at the examples. Add the same endings to each word to create new words.

Ex. walk   walks   walking
                   _____   _____

1. talk   _____   _____

Ex. boss   bosses   bossing
                   _____   _____

2. toss   _____   _____

Directions: Look at each word. Find the related words in the Word Bank. Write the words on the correct lines.

> **Word Bank**
>
> walkway   fell
>
> falling   sidewalk

                   _____   _____

3. fall   _____   _____

                   _____   _____

4. walk   _____   _____

Name: _____ **Date:** _____

Directions: Write each word in the correct column.

Word Bank				
ball	call	fall	jaw	lawn
mall	talk	walk	wall	yawn

Nouns (This is a _____.)	Verbs (I can _____.)

Nouns are naming words. People, places, and things are nouns. Verbs are action words. They name something a person or object does.

Name: _____ **Date:** _____

Directions: Use a word from the Word Bank to complete each analogy.

Analogies

Word Bank

ball	fall	lawn
saw	tall	walk

1. **hear** is to **heard** as **see** is to _____

2. **hockey** is to **puck** as **soccer** is to _____

3. **fast** is to **run** as **slow** is to _____

4. **cut** is to **hair** as **mow** is to _____

5. **summer** is to **winter** as **spring** is to _____

6. **small** is to **big** as **short** is to _____

UNIT 32

R-Controlled Vowels with ar

Focus

This week's focus is one-syllable words that contain *ar*.

Helpful Hint

All the words on this list contain an /ar/ pattern. When *r* comes after a vowel, it gives the vowel a new sound that is neither short nor long. R-controlled vowels are *ar*, *er*, *ir*, *or*, and *ur*. Notice that *r* cannot say its name, or /er/, without the help of a vowel.

➤ are

➤ arm

➤ bar

➤ cart

➤ dark

➤ hard

➤ park

➤ part

➤ star

➤ yard

See page 7 for additional spelling activities.

Name: _____ **Date:** _____

Directions: Use a word from the Word Bank to complete each sentence.

Word Bank		
are	cart	dark
part	star	yard

_____

1. Would you like to save _____ of your sandwich for later?

_____

2. Two bunnies hopped across our _____ yesterday.

_____

3. When _____ you leaving for the store?

_____

4. We came in for dinner when it got _____ outside.

_____

5. Can I push the _____ around the supermarket?

_____

6. I wished on a _____ last night.

Name: _____ **Date:** _____

Directions: Say the word that names each picture. Tap out the sounds in the word. Write the letter or letters that matches each sound in a separate box.

1.

2.

3.

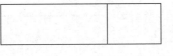

4.

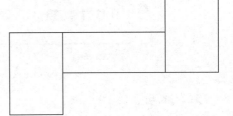

Directions: Write one of the words two times.

_____   _____

_ _ _ _ _ _ _ _ _ _ _ _ _ _ _   _ _ _ _ _ _ _ _ _ _ _ _ _ _ _

Name: _____ **Date:** _____

Directions: Use words from the Word Bank to complete each section.

Word Bank		
arm	cart	dark
hard	park	star

Synonym	Antonym
_____	_____
1. basket _____	3. easy _____
_____	_____
2. playground _____	4. light _____

Write a word that fits each category.

_____

5. leg, foot, hand, _____

_____

6. moon, sun, planet, _____

 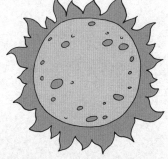 

Name: _____ **Date:** _____

Directions: Answer each question in a complete sentence. Use the bold word in each answer.

1. Why are some kids afraid of the **dark**?

_____

- -

_____

- -

_____

2. Why does the **cart** have four wheels?

_____

- -

_____

- -

_____

3. What is your favorite **park**?

_____

- -

_____

- -

_____

Turn the Question Around

Analogies

Name: _____ **Date:** _____

Directions: Use a word from the Word Bank to complete each analogy.

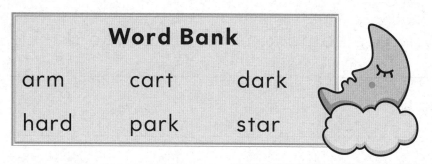

Word Bank

arm	cart	dark
hard	park	star

1. **day** is to **light** as **night** is to _____

2. **foot** is to **leg** as **hand** is to _____

3. **baby** is to **stroller** as **food** is to _____

4. **pillow** is to **soft** as **rock** is to _____

5. **shop** is to **store** as **play** is to _____

6. ♥ is to **heart** as ★ is to _____

UNIT 33

R-Controlled Vowels with *our*, *or*, and *ore*

Focus

This week's focus is one-syllable words that contain *or*, *our*, or *ore*.

Helpful Hint

Notice there are three common ways to make the /or/ sound: *our*, *ore*, and *or*. Usually, *our* and *ore* are used at the end of a word or syllable, while *or* is used in the middle of a word or syllable.

- ➤ born
- ➤ cord
- ➤ corn
- ➤ for
- ➤ fork
- ➤ horn
- ➤ more
- ➤ port
- ➤ sort
- ➤ your

See page 7 for additional spelling activities.

Sentence Completions

Name: _____ **Date:** _____

Directions: Use a word from the Word Bank to complete each sentence.

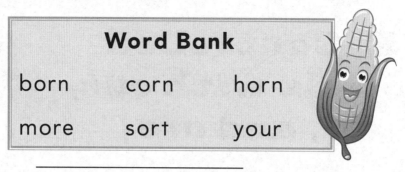

Word Bank

born	corn	horn
more	sort	your

1. My cat was _____ during Hanukkah.

2. You need to _____ the dark and light clothes before you wash them.

3. Dad honked his _____ when a car pulled out in front of him.

4. You may have _____ chicken nuggets when you finish your beans.

5. Mom likes to buy fresh _____ .

6. Did you leave _____ dirty socks on the floor?

Name: _____ **Date:** _____

Directions: Use words from the Word Bank to complete each section.

Word Bank		
cord	corn	fork
more	port	sort

Synonym   **Antonym**

_____   _____

1. harbor _____   3. less _____

                              _____

2. wire _____   4. mix together _____

Write a word that fits each category.

_____

5. carrots, peas, broccoli, _____

_____

6. spoon, knife, chopsticks, _____

Homophones

Name: _____ **Date:** _____

Directions: Homophones sound the same but have different spellings and meanings. Write the correct homophone on each line.

_____
- - - - - - - - - -
1. I baked a cake _____ you!
   (for/four)

_____
- - - - - - - - - -
2. I wish I could _____ across the sky like a bird.
   (soar/sore)

_____
- - - - - - - - - -
3. You may have a hot dog _____ pizza.
   (or/ore)

_____
- - - - - - - - - -
4. My arm was a little _____ after I got a shot.
   (soar/sore)

5. My sister will start preschool when she turns
   _____
   - - - - - - - - - -
   _____ .
   (for/four)

_____
- - - - - - - - - -
6. I _____ my good luck hat to the game.
   (war/wore)

Name: _____ **Date:** _____

Directions: Look at the examples. Add the same endings to each word to create new words.

Ex. storm   storms   storming
                   _____   _____
                   - - - - - - - - - - - -   - - - - - - - - - - - -
1. form   _____   _____

Ex. sport   sports   sporting
                   _____   _____
                   - - - - - - - - - - - -   - - - - - - - - - - - -
2. sort   _____   _____

Directions: Look at each word. Find the related words in the Word Bank. Write the words on the correct lines.

Word Bank	
pitchfork	popcorn
cornbread	forklift

                   _____   _____
                   - - - - - - - - - - - -   - - - - - - - - - - - -
3. fork   _____   _____

                   _____   _____
                   - - - - - - - - - - - -   - - - - - - - - - - - -
4. corn   _____   _____

Inflectional Endings

Name: _____ **Date:** _____

Directions: Use a word from the Word Bank to complete each analogy.

Word Bank

cord	corn	fork
port	sort	your

1. **peel** is to **banana** as **shuck** is to _____

2. **ice cream** is to **spoon** as **cake** is to _____

3. **me** is to **my** as **you** is to _____

4. **trains** is to **rail yard** as **ships** is to _____

5. **put in one pile** is to **combine** as **put in different**

   _____ **piles** is to _____

6. **turn on** is to **switch** as **plug in** is to _____

Analogies

UNIT 34

R-Controlled Vowels with er, ir, and ur

➤ bird

➤ burn

➤ dirt

➤ firm

➤ fur

➤ girl

➤ her

➤ hurt

➤ turn

➤ word

Focus

This week's focus is one-syllable words that contain *er*, *ir*, or *ur*.

Helpful Hint

There are three common ways to make the /er/ sound: *er*, *ir*, and *ur*. Sometimes, *or* also makes an /er/ sound when it comes after *w* (*word*, *worth*).

See page 7 for additional spelling activities.

Name: _____ **Date:** _____

Directions: Use a word from the Word Bank to complete each sentence.

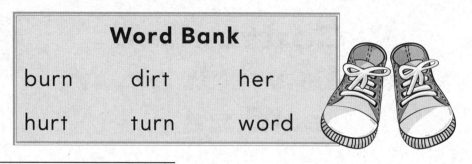

Word Bank		
burn	dirt	her
hurt	turn	word

_____

----

1. I got _____ on my new shoes.

_____

- - - - - - - - - - - -

2. It is my _____ to go down the slide.

_____

- - - - - - - - - - - -

3. I got a _____ on my finger from the hot oven.

_____

- - - - - - - - - - - -

4. The magic _____ is "please."

_____

- - - - - - - - - - - -

5. Does your leg _____ from your fall?

_____

- - - - - - - - - - - -

6. When Mom came home, I gave _____ a big hug.

Name: _____ **Date:** _____

Directions: Say the word that names each picture. Tap out the sounds in the word. Write the letter or letters that matches each sound in a separate box.

1.

2.

3.

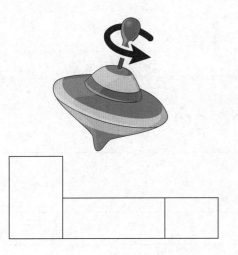

4.

Directions: Write one of the words two times.

_____   _____

_ _ _ _ _ _ _ _ _ _ _ _   _ _ _ _ _ _ _ _ _ _ _ _

_____   _____

Name: _____ **Date:** _____

Directions: Use words from the Word Bank to complete each section.

Word Bank		
bird	dirt	fur
girl	her	turn

Synonym	Antonym
1. soil _____	**3.** boy _____
2. spin _____	**4.** him _____

Write a word that fits each category.

5. hair, feathers, scales, _____

6. fish, mammal, reptile, _____

28629—180 Days of Spelling and Word Study

Name: _____ **Date:** _____

Directions: Look at the examples. Add the same endings to each word to create new words.

Ex. burn   burns   burning
_____   _____

1. turn _____   _____

Ex. hurl   hurls   hurling
_____   _____

2. curl _____   _____

Directions: Look at each word. Find the related words in the Word Bank. Write the words on the correct lines.

Word Bank

hurtful   birdbath

bluebird   hurting

3. bird _____   _____

4. hurt _____   _____

Name: _____ **Date:** _____

Directions: Use a word from the Word Bank to complete each analogy.

Word Bank		
bird	dirt	firm
fur	her	word

1. **he** is to **him** as **she** is to _____

2. **snake** is to **scales** as **dog** is to _____

3. **beach** is to **sand** as **garden** is to _____

4. **3** is to **number** as **three** is to _____

5. **rose** is to **flower** as **parrot** is to _____

6. **banana** is to **mushy** as **apple** is to _____

UNIT 35
–ng Ending

Focus

This week's focus is one-syllable words that end with *–ang*, *–ing*, *–ong*, or *–ung*.

Helpful Hint

All the words on this list contain the *–ng* ending. When *–ng* follows *i*, *o*, or *u*, the vowel makes a short sound (*sing*, *song*, *sung*). When *–ng* follows *a*, the vowel has a long sound (*rang*).

- ➤ **bang**
- ➤ **hang**
- ➤ **hung**
- ➤ **king**
- ➤ **long**
- ➤ **lungs**
- ➤ **ring**
- ➤ **sing**
- ➤ **song**
- ➤ **wing**

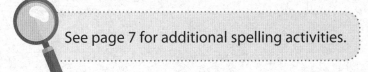

See page 7 for additional spelling activities.

Sentence Completions

Name: _____ **Date:** _____

Directions: Use a word from the Word Bank to complete each sentence.

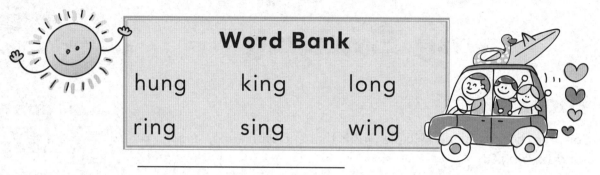

Word Bank

hung	king	long
ring	sing	wing

1. We took a _____ car trip to the beach.

2. Gram _____ my drawings on the wall.

3. We will _____ "Happy Birthday" to Slater at recess.

4. The _____ sat on his throne.

5. The phone started to _____ .

6. The bird hurt its _____ when it fell from the nest.

Name: _____ **Date:** _____

Directions: Use words from the Word Bank to complete each section.

Word Bank		
bang	king	long
ring	sing	wing

Synonym	**Antonym**
1. whack _____	3. short _____
2. hum _____	4. queen _____

Write a word that fits each category.

_____

5. necklace, earring, bracelet, _____

_____

6. fin, leg, flipper, _____

Name: _____ **Date:** _____

Directions: Look at the examples. Add the same endings to each word to create new words.

Ex. ding   dings   dinging

1. sing _____ _____

Ex. hang   hangs   hanging

2. bang _____ _____

Directions: Look at each word. Find the related words in the Word Bank. Write the words on the correct lines.

Word Bank	
earring	longest
longer	rings

3. ring _____ _____

4. long _____ _____

Name: _____ **Date:** _____

Directions: Answer each question in a complete sentence. Use the bold word in each answer.

1. Why do people **sing** in the shower?

_____

_ _

_____

_ _

_____

2. What is your favorite **song**?

_____

_ _

_____

_ _

_____

3. How do you fill your **lungs** with air?

_____

_ _

_____

_ _

_____

Turn the Question Around

Name: _____ **Date:** _____

Directions: Use a word from the Word Bank to complete each analogy.

Analogies

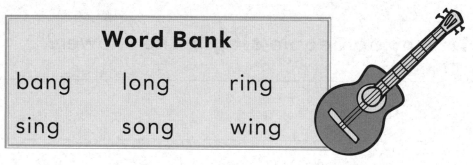

Word Bank

| bang | long | ring |
| sing | song | wing |

1. **fish** is to **fin** as **bird** is to _____

2. **neck** is to **necklace** as **finger** is to _____

3. **guitar** is to **strum** as **drum** is to _____

4. **day** is to **short** as **year** is to _____

5. **read** is to **book** as **sing** is to _____

6. **rang** is to **ring** as **sang** is to _____

28629—180 Days of Spelling and Word Study

UNIT 36
−nk Ending

Focus

This week's focus is one-syllable words that end with −ank, −ink, −onk, or −unk.

Helpful Hint

All the words on this list contain the −nk ending. When −nk follows i, o, or u, the vowel makes a short sound (sink, honk, dunk). When −nk follows a, the vowel has a long sound (bank).

> bank
> dunk
> honk
> junk
> link
> pink
> sank
> sink
> tank
> wink

See page 7 for additional spelling activities.

Name: _____ **Date:** _____

Directions: Use a word from the Word Bank to complete each sentence.

Word Bank		
bank	dunk	honk
junk	pink	sink

_____

- - - - - - - - - -

1. Is _____ your favorite color?

_____

- - - - - - - - - -

2. We have to stop at the _____ to get money.

_____

- - - - - - - - - -

3. Mom likes to _____ donuts in her coffee.

_____

- - - - - - - - - -

4. Go to the _____ to wash your hands.

_____

- - - - - - - - - -

5. I have a pile of _____ to get rid of.

_____

- - - - - - - - - -

6. Let's see if the truck driver will _____ his horn.

Name: _____ **Date:** _____

Directions: Use words from the Word Bank to complete each section.

Word Bank		
bank	honk	hunk
junk	pink	sink

Synonym	Antonym
1. beep _____	3. float _____
2. trash _____	4. tiny piece _____

Write a word that fits each category.

5. red, blue, green, _____

6. store, post office, gas station, _____

Word Sorts

Name: _____ **Date:** _____

Directions: Write each word in the correct column.

Word Bank				
bank	skunk	thank	tank	think
rink	honk	dunk	yank	junk

Nouns (This is a _____.)	Verbs (I can _____.)

28629—180 Days of Spelling and Word Study

Name: _____ Date: _____

Directions: Answer each question in a complete sentence. Use the bold word in each answer.

1. Why do kids stuff **junk** under their beds?

_____

_____

_____

_____

2. Why do people go to the **bank**?

_____

_____

_____

_____

3. Why do drivers **honk** their horns?

_____

_____

_____

_____

Turn the Question Around

Name: _____ **Date:** _____

Directions: Use a word from the Word Bank to complete each analogy.

Word Bank		
bank	honk	pink
sank	sink	tank

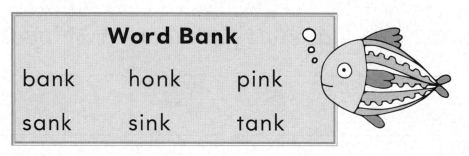

1. **body** is to **tub** as **hands** is to _____

2. **hamster** is to **cage** as **fish** is to _____

3. **food** is to **market** as **money** is to _____

4. **sheep** is to **white** as **pig** is to _____

5. **bell** is to **ring** as **horn** is to _____

6. **drink** is to **drank** as **sink** is to _____

 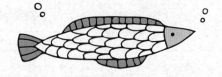 

Answer Key

Week 1 Day 1 (page 12)

1. fan
2. pad
3. cap
4. wax
5. jam
6. pan
7. bag
8. yam
9. nap

Week 1 Day 2 (page 13)

1. c – a – p
2. j – a – m
3. b – a – g
4. f – a – n

Week 1 Day 3 (page 14)

1. h̶   jam
2. m̶   pan
3. t̶   bag
4. m̶   nap

Week 1 Day 4 (page 15)

1. caps
2. yams
3. fans
4. pads

Week 1 Day 5 (page 16)

Sentences should include italicized words.

Week 2 Day 1 (page 18)

1. kids
2. pig
3. lips
4. bib
5. zip
6. dig
7. six
8. ribs
9. fin

Week 2 Day 2 (page 19)

1. p – i – g
2. b – i – b
3. z – i – p
4. d – i – g

Week 2 Day 3 (page 20)

1. p̶   dig
2. l̶   kids
3. ə̶   fin
4. ə̶   six

Week 2 Day 4 (page 21)

1. kids
2. bibs
3. fins
4. pigs

Week 2 Day 5 (page 22)

Sentences should include italicized words.

Week 3 Day 1 (page 24)

1. dog
2. mop
3. rod
4. box
5. log
6. dots
7. pot
8. fox
9. jog

Week 3 Day 2 (page 25)

1. m – o – p
2. p – o – t
3. j – o – g
4. f – o – x

Week 3 Day 3 (page 26)

1. d̶   log
2. ə̶   cop
3. i̶   pot
4. ə̶   mop

Week 3 Day 4 (page 27)

1. boxes
2. foxes
3. pots
4. mops

Week 3 Day 5 (page 28)

Sentences should include italicized words.

Week 4 Day 1 (page 30)

1. gum
2. bug
3. mud
4. bun
5. cup
6. tub
7. rug
8. sun
9. jug

Week 4 Day 2 (page 31)

1. g – u – m
2. r – u – g
3. m – u – d
4. n – u – t

Week 4 Day 3 (page 32)

1. g̶   bus
2. e̶   nut
3. b̶   sun
4. ə̶   cup

Week 4 Day 4 (page 33)

1. buses
2. cups
3. rugs
4. jugs

Week 4 Day 5 (page 34)

Sentences should include italicized words.

Answer Key (cont.)

Week 5 Day 1 (page 36)

1. jet
2. pen
3. bed
4. hen
5. leg
6. web
7. men
8. beg
9. net

Week 5 Day 2 (page 37)

1. l – e – g
2. h – e – n
3. j – e – t
4. w – e – b

Week 5 Day 3 (page 38)

1. n̶   jet
2. a̶   pen
3. g̶   bed
4. B̶   ten

Week 5 Day 4 (page 39)

1. web
2. men
3. leg
4. jet
5. bed
6. pen

Week 5 Day 5 (page 40)

Sentences should include italicized words.

Week 6 Day 1 (page 42)

1. bell
2. doll
3. puff
4. well
5. yell
6. buzz
7. kiss
8. cuff
9. hill

Week 6 Day 2 (page 43)

1. h – i – ll
2. b – e – ll
3. c – u – ff
4. k – i – ss

Week 6 Day 3 (page 44)

1. filled
2. missed
3. passed
4. yelled
5. buzzed
6. kissed
7. puffed
8. tossed

Week 6 Day 4 (page 45)

1. hid
2. fed
3. did
4. sat
5. had
6. ran
7. bit
8. got

Week 6 Day 5 (page 46)

1. hill
2. bell
3. buzz
4. doll
5. yell
6. kiss

Week 7 Day 1 (page 48)

1. rocks
2. duck
3. sack
4. puck
5. lock
6. sock
7. back
8. kick
9. neck

Week 7 Day 2 (page 49)

1. s – o – ck
2. l – o – ck
3. p – u – ck
4. d – u – ck

Week 7 Day 3 (page 50)

1. packed
2. kicked
3. licked
4. tucked
5. locked
6. picked
7. ducked
8. pecked

Week 7 Day 4 (page 51)

Responses should be phrased as the correct sentence types.

Week 7 Day 5 (page 52)

1. back
2. kick
3. lick
4. duck
5. neck
6. deck

Week 8 Day 1 (page 54)

1. chin
2. dish
3. ship
4. rash
5. chick
6. shell
7. shin
8. chip
9. fish

Answer Key (cont.)

Week 8 Day 2 (page 55)

1. sh – i – p
2. d – i – sh
3. ch – i – ck
4. ch – i – n

Week 8 Day 3 (page 56)

1. chicks
2. shells
3. chips
4. ships

Week 8 Day 4 (page 57)

Responses should be phrased as the correct sentence types.

Week 8 Day 5 (page 58)

1. dish
2. ship
3. chick
4. shell
5. rash
6. fish

Week 9 Day 1 (page 60)

1. path
2. with
3. when
4. than
5. thick
6. this

Week 9 Day 2 (page 61)

Soft, unvoiced *th*: bath, math, thick, thin, with
Harder, voiced *th*: than, that, then, them, this

Week 9 Day 3 (page 62)

1. path
2. math
3. thin
4. this
5. thick
6. when

Week 9 Day 4 (page 63)

Responses should be phrased as the correct sentence types.

Week 9 Day 5 (page 64)

1. bath
2. thick
3. math
4. path
5. thin
6. when

Week 10 Day 1 (page 66)

1. vase
2. take
3. ate
4. base
5. save
6. chase

Week 10 Day 2 (page 67)

1. v – a – s – <u>e</u>
2. r – a – k – <u>e</u>
3. s – a – v – <u>e</u>
4. g – a – t – <u>e</u>

Week 10 Day 3 (page 68)

1. missing
2. passing
3. yelling
4. filling
5. shaping
6. making
7. chasing
8. saving

Week 10 Day 4 (page 69)

Responses should be phrased as the correct sentence types.

Week 10 Day 5 (page 70)

1. rake
2. vase
3. male
4. ate
5. gate
6. cave

Week 11 Day 1 (page 72)

1. pile
2. hide
3. bike
4. shine
5. bite
6. time

Week 11 Day 2 (page 73)

1. b – i – k – <u>e</u>
2. t – i – m – <u>e</u>
3. f – i – r – <u>e</u>
4. l – i – m – <u>e</u>

Week 11 Day 3 (page 74)

1. hiding
2. diving
3. riding
4. biting
5. wiped
6. whined
7. piled
8. dined

Week 11 Day 4 (page 75)

Responses should be phrased as the correct sentence types.

Week 11 Day 5 (page 76)

1. bike
2. fire
3. shine
4. lime
5. chime
6. bite

Week 12 Day 1 (page 78)

1. joke
2. use
3. nose
4. robe
5. rule
6. rose

Week 12 Day 2 (page 79)

1. h – o – m – <u>e</u>
2. n – o – s – <u>e</u>
3. r – o – s – <u>e</u>
4. r – o – b – <u>e</u>

Answer Key (cont.)

Week 12 Day 3 (page 80)

1. ruling
2. joking
3. using
4. dozing
5. hoped
6. voted
7. tuned
8. poked

Week 12 Day 4 (page 81)

Responses should be phrased as the correct sentence types.

Week 12 Day 5 (page 82)

1. nose
2. home
3. cute
4. rose
5. robe
6. tube

Week 13 Day 1 (page 84)

1. some
2. come
3. have
4. done
5. give
6. live

Week 13 Day 2 (page 85)

1. gone
2. done
3. some
4. have
5. give
6. come
7. love
8. none

Week 13 Day 3 (page 86)

1. coming
2. giving
3. having
4. living
5. rode
6. gave
7. came
8. had

Week 13 Day 4 (page 87)

Responses should be phrased as the correct sentence types.

Week 13 Day 5 (page 88)

1. one
2. love
3. live
4. give
5. none
6. some

Week 14 Day 1 (page 90)

1. page
2. rice
3. nice
4. ice
5. race
6. huge

Week 14 Day 2 (page 91)

1. c – a – g – <u>e</u>
2. i – c – <u>e</u>
3. r – i – c – <u>e</u>
4. r – a – c – <u>e</u>

Week 14 Day 3 (page 92)

1. face
2. ice
3. pace
4. nice
5. huge
6. rage
7. rice
8. ace

Week 14 Day 4 (page 93)

1. races, racing
2. faces, facing
3. nicest, nicely
4. iceberg, icebox

Week 14 Day 5 (page 94)

1. cage
2. rice
3. huge
4. face
5. race
6. rage

Week 15 Day 1 (page 96)

1. sled
2. flag
3. glass
4. glad
5. slip
6. class

Week 15 Day 2 (page 97)

1. f – l – a – g
2. s – l – e – d
3. g – l – a – ss
4. c – l – a – p

Week 15 Day 3 (page 98)

1. slip
2. clap
3. glad
4. plus
5. glass
6. sled

Week 15 Day 4 (page 99)

1. clapping
2. humming
3. slipping
4. sledding
5. flipped
6. flagged
7. slapped
8. slammed

Week 15 Day 5 (page 100)

1. clap
2. plus
3. glass
4. sled
5. glad
6. slip

Answer Key *(cont.)*

Week 16 Day 1 (page 102)

1. stuff
2. still
3. snap
4. stop
5. swim
6. smell

Week 16 Day 2 (page 103)

1. s – m – e – ll
2. s – w – i – m
3. s – t – e – m
4. s – t – o – p

Week 16 Day 3 (page 104)

1. smell
2. spot
3. stop
4. still
5. stem
6. snap

Week 16 Day 4 (page 105)

1. stopping
2. swimming
3. spitting
4. snapping
5. scabbed
6. stopped
7. snapped
8. spotted

Week 16 Day 5 (page 106)

1. smell
2. stem
3. stop
4. snap
5. spot
6. swim

Week 17 Day 1 (page 108)

1. grill
2. frog
3. grass
4. drop
5. crab
6. from

Week 17 Day 2 (page 109)

1. f – r – o – g
2. c – r – a – b
3. d – r – e – ss
4. g – r – i – ll

Week 17 Day 3 (page 110)

1. dress
2. press
3. trap
4. from
5. grill
6. crab

Week 17 Day 4 (page 111)

1. bragging
2. dropping
3. trapping
4. grabbing
5. dripped
6. trimmed
7. trapped
8. dropped

Week 17 Day 5 (page 112)

1. frog
2. grill
3. grass
4. dress
5. from
6. trap

Week 18 Day 1 (page 114)

1. hay
2. way
3. say
4. pay
5. bay
6. day

Week 18 Day 2 (page 115)

1. h – ay
2. r – ay
3. w – ay
4. s – ay

Week 18 Day 3 (page 116)

1. pay
2. say
3. day
4. may
5. they
6. hay

Week 18 Day 4 (page 117)

1. pays, paying
2. says, saying
3. daylight, daydream
4. stingray, x-ray

Week 18 Day 5 (page 118)

1. pay
2. hay
3. ray
4. they
5. day
6. way

Week 19 Day 1 (page 120)

1. wait
2. aid
3. aim
4. paid
5. gain
6. mail

Week 19 Day 2 (page 121)

1. h – ai – r
2. r – ai – n
3. n – ai – l
4. t – ai – l

Answer Key *(cont.)*

Week 19 Day 3 (page 122)

1. aid
2. aim
3. wait
4. gain
5. rain
6. nail

Week 19 Day 4 (page 123)

1. mails, mailing
2. rains, raining
3. fingernail, toenail
4. hairspray, hairbrush

Week 19 Day 5 (page 124)

1. hair
2. nail
3. gain
4. air
5. rain
6. mail

Week 20 Day 1 (page 126)

1. read
2. beak
3. teach
4. each
5. seal
6. hear

Week 20 Day 2 (page 127)

1. l – ea – f
2. b – ea – k
3. s – ea – l
4. ea – t

Week 20 Day 3 (page 128)

1. hear
2. each
3. teach
4. real
5. leaf
6. seal

Week 20 Day 4 (page 129)

1. leaped
2. healed
3. heated
4. leaned
5. ate
6. heard
7. led
8. taught

Week 20 Day 5 (page 130)

1. leaf
2. beak
3. hear
4. eat
5. heat
6. read

Week 21 Day 1 (page 132)

1. feed
2. wheel
3. meet
4. feel
5. queen
6. keep

Week 21 Day 2 (page 133)

1. feel
2. feed
3. queen
4. keep
5. week
6. wheel

Week 21 Day 3 (page 134)

1. peeked
2. peeled
3. needed
4. wheeled
5. kept
6. fed
7. met
8. felt

Week 21 Day 4 (page 135)

Responses should be phrased as the correct sentence types.

Week 21 Day 5 (page 136)

1. week
2. wheel
3. queen
4. feel
5. meet
6. keep

Week 22 Day 1 (page 138)

1. load
2. soap
3. goal
4. coat
5. goat
6. road

Week 22 Day 2 (page 139)

1. coat
2. road
3. moan
4. load
5. goal
6. soap

Week 22 Day 3 (page 140)

1. moans, moaning
2. foams, foaming
3. railroad, roadwork
4. sailboat, tugboat

Week 22 Day 4 (page 141)

Responses should be phrased as the correct sentence types.

Week 22 Day 5 (page 142)

1. coat
2. soap
3. soak
4. road
5. goat
6. goal

Week 23 Day 1 (page 144)

1. grow
2. bow
3. mow
4. tow
5. row
6. low

Answer Key (cont.)

Week 23 Day 2 (page 145)

1. s – n – ow
2. r – ow
3. t – oe
4. b – ow

Week 23 Day 3 (page 146)

1. row
2. show
3. foe
4. low
5. snow
6. toe

Week 23 Day 4 (page 147)

1. so
2. know
3. dough
4. no
5. sew
6. toe

Week 23 Day 5 (page 148)

1. low
2. mow
3. bow
4. toe
5. foe
6. tow

Week 24 Day 1 (page 150)

1. sky
2. pie
3. dry
4. try
5. lie
6. tie

Week 24 Day 2 (page 151)

1. t – ie
2. p – ie
3. f – l – y
4. c – r – y

Week 24 Day 3 (page 152)

1. try
2. tie
3. dry
4. cry
5. pie
6. why

Week 24 Day 4 (page 153)

1. dies, dying
2. lies, lying
3. dryer, dried
4. flies, butterfly

Week 24 Day 5 (page 154)

1. pie
2. sky
3. cry
4. dry
5. tie
6. fly

Week 25 Day 1 (page 156)

1. fight
2. might
3. high
4. light
5. right
6. sigh

Week 25 Day 2 (page 157)

1. fight
2. right
3. high
4. light
5. thigh
6. sight

Week 25 Day 3 (page 158)

1. hi
2. night
3. by
4. high
5. write
6. bye

Week 25 Day 4 (page 159)

Sentences should include bolded words.

Week 25 Day 5 (page 160)

1. night
2. light
3. fight
4. high
5. sight
6. right

Week 26 Day 1 (page 162)

1. mood
2. cool
3. pool
4. food
5. noon
6. loop

Week 26 Day 2 (page 163)

1. roof
2. soon
3. cool
4. noon
5. pool
6. moon

Week 26 Day 3 (page 164)

1. cools, cooling
2. rooms, rooming
3. moonlight, moons
4. rooftop, sunroof

Week 26 Day 4 (page 165)

Sentences should include bolded words.

Week 26 Day 5 (page 166)

1. noon
2. cool
3. food
4. moon
5. pool
6. tool

Answer Key (cont.)

Week 27 Day 1 (page 168)

1. few
2. new
3. flew
4. blue
5. glue
6. dew

Week 27 Day 2 (page 169)

1. glue
2. dew
3. few
4. new
5. blue
6. stew

Week 27 Day 3 (page 170)

1. due
2. too
3. dew
4. two
5. to
6. do

Week 27 Day 4 (page 171)

1. chews, chewing
2. glues, gluing
3. bluebird, blueberry
4. newer, newest

Week 27 Day 5 (page 172)

1. glue
2. blue
3. flew
4. new
5. dew
6. due

Week 28 Day 1 (page 174)

1. push
2. took
3. book
4. put
5. good
6. wood

Week 28 Day 2 (page 175)

1. pull
2. wood
3. full
4. good
5. look
6. foot

Week 28 Day 3 (page 176)

1. looked
2. cooked
3. pulled
4. pushed
5. took
6. shook
7. stood
8. flew

Week 28 Day 4 (page 177)

Sentences should include bolded words.

Week 28 Day 5 (page 178)

1. foot
2. wood
3. pull
4. book
5. took
6. look

Week 29 Day 1 (page 180)

1. gown
2. out
3. about
4. mouth
5. how
6. down

Week 29 Day 2 (page 181)

1. m – ou – th
2. d – ow – n
3. g – ow – n
4. c – ou – ch

Week 29 Day 3 (page 182)

1. town
2. couch
3. out
4. loud
5. how
6. mouth

Week 29 Day 4 (page 183)

1. towns
2. mouths
3. couches
4. gowns
5. nouns
6. cows
7. clouds
8. pouches

Week 29 Day 5 (page 184)

1. mouth
2. down
3. town
4. loud
5. gown
6. couch

Week 30 Day 1 (page 186)

1. join
2. boy
3. soil
4. joy
5. coin
6. oil

Week 30 Day 2 (page 187)

1. soil
2. oil
3. join
4. joy
5. coin
6. foil

Week 30 Day 3 (page 188)

1. boils, boiling
2. joins, joining
3. enjoy, joyful
4. oils, oiled

Answer Key (cont.)

Week 30 Day 4 (page 189)

Sentences should include bolded words.

Week 30 Day 5 (page 190)

1. soil
2. boy
3. boil
4. joy
5. coil
6. toy

Week 31 Day 1 (page 192)

1. talk
2. ball
3. toss
4. walk
5. loss
6. saw

Week 31 Day 2 (page 193)

1. lawn
2. toss
3. loss
4. tall
5. fall
6. talk

Week 31 Day 3 (page 194)

1. talks, talking
2. tosses, tossing
3. falling, fell
4. walkway, sidewalk

Week 31 Day 4 (page 195)

Nouns: ball, wall, jaw, lawn, mall
Verbs: walk, talk, call, yawn, fall

Week 31 Day 5 (page 196)

1. saw
2. ball
3. walk
4. lawn
5. fall
6. tall

Week 32 Day 1 (page 198)

1. part
2. yard
3. are
4. dark
5. cart
6. star

Week 32 Day 2 (page 199)

1. ar – m
2. p – ar – k or y – ar – d
3. s – t – ar
4. c – ar – t

Week 32 Day 3 (page 200)

1. yard
2. park
3. hard
4. dark
5. arm
6. star

Week 32 Day 4 (page 201)

Sentences should include bolded words.

Week 32 Day 5 (page 202)

1. dark
2. arm
3. cart
4. hard
5. park
6. star

Week 33 Day 1 (page 204)

1. born
2. sort
3. horn
4. more
5. corn
6. your

Week 33 Day 2 (page 205)

1. port
2. cord
3. more
4. sort
5. corn
6. fork

Week 33 Day 3 (page 206)

1. for
2. soar
3. or
4. sore
5. four
6. wore

Week 33 Day 4 (page 207)

1. forms, forming
2. sorts, sorting
3. pitchfork, forklift
4. popcorn, cornbread

Week 33 Day 5 (page 208)

1. corn
2. fork
3. your
4. port
5. sort
6. cord

Week 34 Day 1 (page 210)

1. dirt
2. turn
3. burn
4. word
5. hurt
6. her

Week 34 Day 2 (page 211)

1. g – ir – l
2. b – ir – d
3. t – ur – n
4. h – ur – t

Answer Key (cont.)

Week 34 Day 3 (page 212)

1. dirt
2. turn
3. girl
4. her
5. fur
6. bird

Week 34 Day 4 (page 213)

1. turns, turning
2. curls, curling
3. birdbath, bluebird
4. hurtful, hurting

Week 34 Day 5 (page 214)

1. her
2. fur
3. dirt
4. word
5. bird
6. firm

Week 35 Day 1 (page 216)

1. long
2. hung
3. sing
4. king
5. ring
6. wing

Week 35 Day 2 (page 217)

1. bang
2. sing
3. long
4. king
5. ring
6. wing

Week 35 Day 3 (page 218)

1. sings, singing
2. bangs, banging
3. earring, rings
4. longest, longer

Week 35 Day 4 (page 219)

Sentences should include bolded words.

Week 35 Day 5 (page 220)

1. wing
2. ring
3. bang
4. long
5. song
6. sing

Week 36 Day 1 (page 222)

1. pink
2. bank
3. dunk
4. sink
5. junk
6. honk

Week 36 Day 2 (page 223)

1. honk
2. junk
3. sink
4. hunk
5. pink
6. bank

Week 36 Day 3 (page 224)

Nouns: bank, skunk, tank, rink, junk
Verbs: thank, think, honk, dunk, yank

Week 36 Day 4 (page 225)

Sentences should include bolded words.

Week 36 Day 5 (page 226)

1. sink
2. tank
3. bank
4. pink
5. honk
6. sank

Unit Assessments

At the end of each unit, use the corresponding quiz to determine what students have learned. Ask students to spell the two words. Then, have students write the sentence. Say the words and sentence slowly, repeating as often as needed. The bolded words were studied in the unit.

Unit	Phonetic Pattern	Words	Sentence
1	short *a* words	ham, sad	The **jam** is in the **bag**.
2	short *i* words	fix, lids	Did the **kids quit**?
3	short *o* words	fog, rod	Dad likes to **jog** to his **job**.
4	short *u* words	dug, hut	Is that a **bug** in your **cup**?
5	short *e* words	wet, yet	The **men** hit the **bed** in the **jet**.
6	bonus letters	fuzz, mess	The **doll** fell down the **hill**.
7	–*ck* ending	peck, tuck	Nick has lots of rocks on the **back deck**.
8	consonant digraphs *ch* and *sh*	chat, shed	We go to the dock to **fish** and check for **shells**.
9	consonant digraphs *th* and *wh*	math, thud	**When** did you get **this bath** mat?
10	silent *e* with *a*	bake, shame	Jake was **late** so he had to **chase** the bus.
11	silent *e* with *i*	dime, wide	My **time** at the lake was quite fun!
12	silent *e* with *o* and *u*	cube, hose	Do you have the same **rules** at **home**?
13	silent *e* rule breakers	glove, shove	**Give** me the name of **one** book you **love**.
14	soft *c* and soft *g* words	dice, age	Five **huge** mice sat in the **cage**.
15	initial blends with *l*	flat, plug	I am **glad** we made a **flag** for the club.
16	initial blends with *s*	skip, swell	**Stop**! It is not safe to **swim** in that **spot**.
17	initial blends with *r*	draw, trim	Did you **drop** your black pen in the **grass**?
18	long *a* vowel team *ay*	tray, stay	I hope **they** will **pay** you back some **day**.
19	long *a* vowel team *ai*	laid, pain	Did you **wait** for the **mail** in the **rain**?
20	long *e* vowel team *ea*	meat, reach	Sit in your seat while I **teach** you to **read**.
21	long *e* vowel team *ee*	seep, weed	You may **keep** my **queen** doll for one **week**.

Unit Assessments *(cont.)*

Unit	Phonetic Pattern	Words	Sentence
22	long *o* vowel team *oa*	coal, toad	Put on your **coat** or the rain will **soak** you.
23	long *o* vowel teams *oe* and *ow*	crow, doe	Will you **show** me where to find **snow**?
24	long *i* patterns *ie* and *y*	shy, spy	**Why** did you **tie** my laces to the bed?
25	long *i* pattern *igh*	flight, bright	My dog and your cat **might** get in a **fight**.
26	long *u* pattern *oo*	fool, hoop	I sit in my **room** when I am in a bad **mood**.
27	long *u* vowel teams *ue* and *ew*	grew, sue	Mike ate a **few** bites of his **stew**.
28	words with schwa	dull, shook	Did you **put** the **books** back in the box?
29	*ou* and *ow* diphthongs	chow, pout	I have to get **out** of this **town now**!
30	*oi* and *oy* diphthongs	soy, toil	Some **coins** and a **toy** were in the **soil**.
31	words with /*aw*/ sound	boss, raw	We can **talk** while we **walk** to the mall.
32	*r*-controlled vowels with *ar*	bark, farm	You can play in the **yard** when it gets **dark**.
33	*r*-controlled vowels with *our*, *or*, and *ore*	short, torn	Can you **sort** the **forks** and spoons?
34	*r*-controlled vowels with *er*, *ir*, and *ur*	stir, curl	The **girl** got **hurt** when she fell in the **dirt**.
35	–*ng* ending	rang, thing	I **hung** wet stuff on the **long** line.
36	–*nk* ending	bunk, think	Why did you **dunk** your hands in the fish **tank**?

Spelling Categories

Spelling Category	Spelling Pattern	Unit
Short Vowels	short *a* words	1
	short *i* words	2
	short *o* words	3
	short *u* words	4
	short *e* words	5
Consonant Digraphs and Blends	bonus letters	6
	–*ck* ending	7
	consonant digraphs *ch* and *sh*	8
	consonant digraphs *th* and *wh*	9
	initial blends with *l*	15
	initial blends with *s*	16
	initial blends with *r*	17
	–*ng* ending	35
	–*nk* ending	36
Silent and Soft Letters	silent *e* with *a*	10
	silent *e* with *i*	11
	silent *e* with *o* and *u*	12
	silent *e* rule breakers	13
	soft *c* and soft *g* words	14
Long Vowels	long *a* vowel team *ay*	18
	long *a* vowel team *ai*	19
	long *e* vowel team *ea*	20
	long *e* vowel team *ee*	21
	long *o* vowel team *oa*	22
	long *o* vowel teams *oe* and *ow*	23
	long *i* patterns *ie* and *y*	24
	long *i* pattern *igh*	25
	long *u* pattern *oo*	26
	long *u* vowel teams *ue* and *ew*	27
Ambiguous Vowels	words with schwa	28
	ou and *ow* diphthongs	29
	oi and *oy* diphthongs	30
	words with /*aw*/ sound	31
R-Controlled Vowels	r-controlled vowels with *ar*	32
	r-controlled vowels with *our*, *or*, and *ore*	33
	r-controlled vowels with *er*, *ir*, and *ur*	34

Digital Resources

Accessing the Digital Resources

The digital resources can be downloaded by following these steps:

1. Go to **www.tcmpub.com/digital**

2. Sign in or create an account.

3. Click **Redeem Content** and enter the ISBN number, located on page 2 and the back cover, into the appropriate field on the website.

4. Respond to the prompts using the book to view your account and available digital content.

5. Choose the digital resources you would like to download. You can download all the files at once, or you can download a specific group of files.

ISBN:
9781425833091

Please note: Some files provided for download have large file sizes. Download times for these larger files will vary based on your download speed.

Contents of the Digital Resources

Teaching Resources Folder

- Additional Spelling Activities (page 7)

- Additional Word Lists (below, on, and above grade level)

- Unit Overview Pages

Assessments Folder

- Analysis Charts separated by spelling category

- Unit Assessments (pages 237–238)

- Assessment Reproducible